A2

English for SOCIALIZING AND SMALL TALK

SHORT COURSE SERIES

Annie Cornford

This book is also available online on
www.scook.de/eb

Please accept the terms and conditions to use the eBook.

Book Code: **2qgbe-zf7xt**

Impressum

Verfasser:	Annie Cornford
Berater:	Roy Bicknell, Amsterdam
	Anne Hodgson, Berlin
Projektleitung:	Andreas Göbel
Redaktion:	Anna Batrla, Meike Kolle
Außenredaktion:	Christine House, Berlin
Redaktionelle Mitarbeit:	Janan Barksdale, Zsuzsa Parádi
Bildredaktion:	Rani Kumar, Berlin
Layoutkonzept:	finedesign, Berlin
Technische Umsetzung:	zweiband.media, Berlin
Umschlagsgestaltung:	Studio SYBERG, Berlin; Jan Haux / Pepe Jürgens, Berlin

Quellen

Titelfoto © Fotolia, Africa Studio | **S. 4** v. o.: © Shutterstock, michaeljung; © Shutterstock, Tyler Olson; © Shutterstock, dotshock; © Shutterstock, lightwavemedia; © Shutterstock, ProStockStudio | **S. 5** v. o.: © Shutterstock, bikeriderlondon; © Shutterstock, Robert Kneschke; © Shutterstock, Valeria73 | **S. 6** © Shutterstock, michaeljung | **S. 7** © Fotolia, Studio Mike | **S. 9** © Shutterstock, NAN728 | **S. 12** © Shutterstock, Tyler Olson | **S. 13** © Shutterstock, wavebreakmedia | **S. 17** © Shutterstock, Rawpixel.com | **S. 18** © Shutterstock, dotshock | **S. 19** © Shutterstock, OPOLJA | **S. 20** © Shutterstock, bikeriderlondon | **S. 23** © Shutterstock, BLePister | **S. 24** © Shutterstock, lightwavemedia | **S. 25** © Shutterstock, Daxiao Productions | **S. 27** © Shutterstock, Candybox Images | **S. 30** © Shutterstock, ProStockStudio | **S. 31** © Shutterstock, Oleg Senkov | **S. 35** © Shutterstock, iQoncept | **S. 36** © Shutterstock, bikeriderlondon | **S. 38** © Shutterstock, OrelPhoto | **S. 42** oben: © Shutterstock, Robert Kneschke; unten: © Oxford Designers & Illustrators | **S. 44** © Shutterstock, racorn | **S. 47** © Shutterstock, michaeljung | **S. 48** © Fotolia, davis | **S. 49** © Shutterstock, goodluz | **S. 50** © Shutterstock, Sergey Nivens | **S. 51** © Shutterstock, goodluz | S. 53 © Shutterstock, Jesus Sanz

www.cornelsen.de

1. Auflage, 1. Druck 2016

Alle Drucke dieser Auflage sind inhaltlich unverändert und können im Unterricht nebeneinander verwendet werden.

© 2016 Cornelsen Schulverlage GmbH, Berlin

Das Werk und seine Teile sind urheberrechtlich geschützt. Jede Nutzung in anderen als den gesetzlich zugelassenen Fällen bedarf der vorherigen schriftlichen Einwilligung des Verlages. .

Hinweis zu den §§ 46, 52 a UrhG: Weder das Werk noch seine Teile dürfen ohne eine solche Einwilligung eingescannt und in ein Netzwerk eingestellt oder sonst öffentlich zugänglich gemacht werden.

Dies gilt auch für Intranets von Schulen und sonstigen Bildungseinrichtungen.

Druck: Mohn Media Mohndruck, Gütersloh

ISBN: 978-3-464-20576-1

PEFC zertifiziert
Dieses Produkt stammt aus nachhaltig bewirtschafteten Wäldern und kontrollierten Quellen.
www.pefc.de

English for Socializing and Small Talk im Überblick

Willkommen zu Ihrem A2 Short Course *English for Socializing and Small Talk*. Das Ziel dieses Buches ist es, Ihnen die Sicherheit und das Werkzeug für das freie Sprechen auf Englisch an die Hand zu geben. Dabei orientieren wir uns an allerlei Geschäftssituationen, die in der globalen Welt vermehrt auftreten. In acht Units entwickeln Sie die Fertigkeit und das notwendige Vokabular, um mit solch relevanten Themen wie bspw. Besucher empfangen, über Pläne sprechen oder sich mit Kollegen unterhalten kompetent umzugehen.

- Die acht Units bringen Ihnen Schritt für Schritt auf jeweils sechs Seiten das wichtigste Vokabular und die grundlegenden Sprachmuster näher.

- Die Units bauen auf realistischen Szenarios auf, die auf einer Reihe von Geschäftsfeldern basieren und übliche Situationen widerspiegeln, in denen es zu Small Talk kommen kann. In vielfältigen Übungen setzen Sie die gelernten Fertigkeiten und Vokabeln dann ein und festigen das Gelernte somit.

- Die für Small Talk wichtigsten Formulierungen eignen Sie sich aktiv mithilfe der *Phrase boxes* an und können diese am Ende jeder Unit noch einmal in den *Key phrases* wiederholen.

- Mit *Over to you* baut das Buch auf Ihren Small-Talk-Kenntnissen auf und fördert diese. Durch Partnerübungen werden Sie dazu animiert, miteinander zu kommunizieren.

- Jede Unit endet mit *Last but not least*, einem kurzem Text zum Thema, der ausgiebig zu Diskussionen einlädt.

- Authentische Dialoge auf der beiliegenden CD schulen Ihr Hörverstehen. Eine Reihe von Akzenten spiegelt die internationale Geschäftswelt wider und ermöglicht es Ihnen, sich realitätsnahen Situationen auszusetzen.

- Im Anhang finden Sie eine umfassende Liste mit den wichtigsten Formulierungen. Auf diese können Sie jederzeit zurückgreifen, egal ob im Unterricht oder außerhalb. Zusätzlich gibt es dort die Transkripte für die Höraufgaben, einen Lösungsschlüssel und eine A-Z Wortliste.

Die Autorin und die Redaktion wünschen Ihnen viel Freude und Erfolg mit *English for Socializing and Small Talk*! Wir hoffen, dass es Ihnen auf Ihrem Weg zu mühelosem Small Talk auf Englisch einen gelungenen Beitrag leisten wird.

Inhaltsverzeichnis

1 Meeting a visitor

- Greeting someone you know
- Greeting someone you don't know
- Saying sorry
- Offering help
- Making small talk about the trip

welcome good to see you
my pleasure how are you?
how was your trip? that's ok
are these your bags?

Page 6

2 Talking about plans

- Making visitors feel welcome
- Saying you want to freshen up
- Talking about travel options
- Explaining the schedule
- Asking questions about the schedule

something to drink?
I'll pick you up first appointment
freshen up is it far from here?
grab some lunch

Page 12

3 Welcoming a visitor to the company

- Arriving at a company
- Giving directions around the office
- Checking understanding

come this way elevator
you're welcome
a cup of tea what do you mean?
lovely to see you again

Page 18

4 Chatting with colleagues

- Introducing colleagues
- Welcoming a new colleague
- Talking about people you both know
- Talking about where you are from
- Departments

where are you from?
good to see you
have you two met? in touch
R&D sales I'm good,
HR   thank you!

Page 24

5 Entertaining a visitor

- Asking for sightseeing tips
- Giving sightseeing tips
- Asking for directions
- Giving directions
- Inviting
- Accepting or refusing invitations

excuse me
join us for dinner any tips
how about tomorrow?
I'm lost I'm sorry but I'm busy
next to the hotel

Page 30

6 Eating out

- Talking about what to eat
- Helping with the menu
- Ordering a meal
- Paying for the meal
- Before and after the meal

Page 36

try it don't mention it
enjoy your meal this is on me
vegetarian ready to order
cheers! are you hungry?
I can't eat seafood

7 Making small talk

- Talking about the weather
- Discussing family relationships
- Talking about free-time activities

Page 42

do yoga married
I hate gardening lovely today
grown up separated hobbies
what's the weather like? play cards

8 At a business event

- Starting a conversation
- Taking part in discussions
- Talking about what you do
- Ending a conversation

Page 48

haven't we met before?
nice talking to you networking
take my card
really have to leave now I'm sorry unfortunately

Anhang

Page 54 Transcripts
Page 55 Answer key
Page 59 Key phrases (English–German)
Page 68 A–Z wordlist
Page 72 Tracklist

Symbole und Abkürzungen

🔊 02 Tracknummer
👥 Partnerarbeit
AE amerikanisches Englisch
BE britisches Englisch
sb. somebody (jemand)
sth. something (etwas)

Learning objectives
- Greeting a visitor
  Einen Besucher begrüßen
- Making small talk about the trip
  Sich über die Reise austauschen
- Offering help
  Hilfe anbieten

1 Meeting a visitor

1 ◁02 Read and listen to these short dialogues. Which dialogues are with …

a a person you know? .... b a person you don't know? ....

1
- Hello, I'm Anna Schmidt. It's nice to meet you.
- I'm Dave. Nice to meet you too.

2
- James Miller? Welcome to Berlin. My name's Jan.
- Pleased to meet you, Jan.

3
- Greg! It's good to see you again. How are you?
- I'm fine, thanks. Very good to see you too.

4
- My name's Jens Fuchs.
- Hi, Jens. It's great to meet you. I'm Mary Rosen, but please call me Mary.

How do you usually welcome business partners who come to see you?

> It's nice to <u>meet</u> you.
> = Schön, Sie kennenzulernen.
>
> It's nice to <u>see</u> you (again).
> = Schön, Sie wiederzusehen.

2 ◁03 Harry is welcoming two visitors.
Read and listen to the dialogue. Who knows everybody?

☐ Harry ☐ Helga ☐ Franz

Harry	Helga, it's good to see you again! How are you?
Helga	I'm fine, thanks, Harry. Good to see you too.
Harry	You look very well.
Helga	Thank you. You too!
Harry	Thanks.
Helga	Harry, do you know my colleague Franz Maier? Franz, this is Harry Norton.
Franz	Hello, Harry. It's good to meet you.
Harry	It's nice to meet you too, Franz.

Did you know?
Business people often use first names in English. If the person you meet uses your first name, it is usually safe to use his or her first name too.

English for Socializing and Small Talk

3 🔊 04 Jens is meeting a visitor at the airport. Read and listen to the dialogue. Why is Jens sorry?

a ☐ He forgets his visitor's name.
b ☐ He is late.
c ☐ The weather is bad.
d ☐ The plane was late.

Vocabulary

baggage claim Gepäckausgabe
finally endlich
My pleasure. Keine Ursache.
traffic Verkehr
to worry sich Sorgen machen
You must be Carolyn. Sie sind bestimmt Carolyn.

Jens Hello. You must be Carolyn Scott. Welcome to Frankfurt. My name is Jens Fuchs.
Carolyn It's great to finally meet you, Mr. Fuchs.
Jens You too. Please, just call me Jens. I'm sorry I'm late. The traffic was really bad.
Carolyn That's OK, Jens. I just got here.

I'm sorry I'm late. (not I'm too late)

Jens Oh really? Was your flight late?
Carolyn No, but baggage claim was so slow.
Jens And then you had to wait for me. I'm sorry, Carolyn.
Carolyn Don't worry, it's OK. It's nice of you to meet me here.
Jens My pleasure. You don't know the city, do you?
Carolyn No, this is my first time in Frankfurt.

4 Look at the dialogues in exercises 2 and 3 again and complete the phrases below.

Phrases

Greeting someone you know

It's good to _____¹ again. – You too.

How are you? – _____², thanks. And you?

Greeting someone you don't know

_____³ Frankfurt. _____⁴ is Jens Fuchs.

It's great to _____⁵ you, Mr. Fuchs.

It's nice of you to meet me here. – My _____⁶.

Saying sorry

I'm _____⁷ I'm late.

_____⁸, it's OK.

5 Match the two parts of these phrases.

1 You must be
2 It's great
3 Welcome
4 I'm sorry
5 Baggage claim was
6 It's nice of you

a I'm late.
b to meet me here.
c Sarah Jones.
d to finally meet you.
e to Berlin.
f so slow.

to meet sb. = jdn. kennenlernen + jdn. treffen, abholen

6 🔊 05 Paula has just arrived in Germany. Read and listen to the dialogue. Is this her first time in Stuttgart?

Joe	So, Paula, how was your trip?
Paula	Not so good.
Joe	Oh, was the flight delayed?
Paula	No, but I had to get up very early.
Joe	You must be tired now.
Paula	I'm a bit tired, but I'm OK, thanks. I slept on the plane.
Joe	Have you ever been here before?
Paula	Yes, I have. I was here three years ago.
Joe	Oh, so you know Stuttgart well.
Paula	No, my meetings were all at the airport hotel!
Joe	I see.
Paula	So I can't wait to see the city this time.
Joe	Good. And I'm looking forward to showing you around.
Paula	Thank you, Joe.

> **Vocabulary**
> a bit tired ein bisschen müde
> delayed verspätet
> I can't wait … Ich kann es kaum erwarten, …

> *I'm looking forward to showing you around. (not I'm looking forward to show …)*

7 Read the mini-dialogues. Tick (✓) the correct response.

1 How was your flight?
   a ☐ Fine, thanks.
   b ☐ I was here three years ago.

2 You must be tired now.
   a ☐ No, this is my first time.
   b ☐ No, I'm OK, thank you.

3 Have you ever been to Germany before?
   a ☐ Yes, I'm fine, thanks.
   b ☐ No, this is my first visit.

4 I'm looking forward to showing you around.
   a ☐ That's very nice of you.
   b ☐ That's not great.

> **Did you know?**
> Is this your visitor's first visit? A good way to ask is with "Have you ever … ?" questions: *Have you ever been here / visited our company before?*
> It is friendly to answer with more information than "Yes, I have." or "No, I haven't."
> *Yes, I have. I visited this office a year ago.* or *No, I haven't. But I'm looking forward to seeing it.*

8 Look at the dialogue in exercise 6 again and complete the phrases below.

> **Phrases**
>
> **Making small talk about the trip**
>
> How _____¹? – Fine, thanks. / Not so good.
>
> Was the flight _____²? – No, but I had to get up _____³.
>
> I'm a bit tired, but _____⁴.
>
> _____⁵ before?
>
> – Yes, I have. _____⁶ three years ago.

9 ◁06 Harry is talking to his visitors. Read and listen to the dialogue. Who wants help, Helga or Franz?

Harry	My car's parked outside. Can I help you with your bags?
Helga	No, I can manage, thanks.
Harry	Let me get that suitcase for you.
Helga	No, really. I'm fine, thanks.
Harry	Franz, are those your bags?
Franz	Yes, they are.
Harry	Can I help you?
Franz	It's OK, but could you take this briefcase for me, please?
Harry	Sure, no problem.
Franz	That's great, thank you.

Vocabulary

briefcase Aktentasche
I can manage. Es geht schon.
luggage Gepäck
suitcase Koffer

Talk to a partner about your business trips. How long are they, and how much luggage do you usually take?

10 Look at the dialogue in exercise 9 again and complete the phrases below.

> **Phrases**
>
> **Offering help**
>
> Can I help you with ....¹?
>
> ....² that suitcase for you.
>
> Are those your bags? ... .³ you?

11 Put the words into the correct order to make questions.

1 that | your | luggage | Is ....?

2 bags | help | you | your | I | Can | with ....?

3 you | Could | me | please | for | this | take ....?

Now match the questions to the answers.

a ☐ Sure. No problem.   b ☐ Yes, it is.   c ☐ No, I can manage, thank you.

12 ◁07 Listen to three short dialogues and tick the phrases you hear.

Greeting a visitor

1 a ☐ My name is Erika Schuster.   2 a ☐ It's nice to finally meet you.
   b ☐ I'm Erika Schuster.   b ☐ I'm pleased to meet you.

Offering / Asking for help with luggage

3 a ☐ Can I help you with your luggage?   4 a ☐ Can you help me, please?
   b ☐ Can I help you with your suitcase?   b ☐ Could you take this for me, please?

Making small talk about the trip

5 a ☐ Is this your first time here?   6 a ☐ I can't wait to see everyone again.
   b ☐ Have you been here before?   b ☐ I'm looking forward to seeing everyone again.

Key phrases

Here are some key phrases from the unit. Tick the ones that are useful for you.

Greeting someone you know
- ☐ Hello, it's good to see you (again).
  – (It's) Good to see you too.
- ☐ How are you?
  – I'm fine, thank you. And you?

Greeting someone you don't know
- ☐ James Miller? Welcome to Berlin.
- ☐ My name is Jan.
- ☐ It's nice to meet you (, Jan). – Pleased to meet you (too).
- ☐ It's great to finally meet you. – You too.
- ☐ It is nice of you to meet me here. – My pleasure.

Saying sorry
- ☐ I'm sorry I'm late.
  – That's OK.
- ☐ I am sorry.
  – Don't worry, it's OK.

Meeting a visitor

Offering help
- ☐ Are these your bags?
  – Yes, they are.
- ☐ Can I help you with your suitcase?
  – It's OK, but could you take this briefcase for me, please?
- ☐ Let me get that for you.
  – No, really, I'm fine, thanks.
  – I can manage, thanks.

Making small talk about the trip
- ☐ How was your flight/trip?
  – Fine, thanks.
  – Not so good. The traffic was really bad.
- ☐ You must be tired now.
  – I'm all right, thanks. I slept on the plane.
  – I'm a bit tired but I'm OK, thanks.
- ☐ Have you been here before?
  – No, I haven't. I can't wait to look around. / I'm looking forward to seeing the city.
  – Yes, I have, I was here three years ago.

You will find an English-German list of these phrases on pages 59–60.

Use this space to write your own useful words and phrases.

....

....

....

....

....

Over to you

13 Think of a situation where you are meeting a visitor. Write down how you would do the following.

Greet a person you know: ....

Greet a person you don't know and say who you are: ....

Offer help with their bags: ....

Make small talk about the trip: ....

....

Now work with a partner and practice meeting a visitor. Then change roles and do the activity again. Partner A is the host, Partner B the visitor.

A Greet B.

B Greet A.

A Offer B some help.

B Reply.

A Ask about B's trip.

B Reply.

A Ask if it is B's first visit here.

B Reply.

Last but not least

14 Read these tips on doing business with different cultures.

Doing business with other cultures

When you do business with people from another culture, it's good to know the basic business etiquette of your visitor's country, so take some time to find out about it before meeting them.

In the United States, for example, people are less formal than in Germany, so be friendly but not too friendly on your first meeting.

When you meet Asian visitors for the first time, do not shake hands immediately. Physical contact can make some people unhappy. Japanese business people may shake your hand, but the normal greeting in Japan is the bow. It's best to do what your visitor does.

People from Spain, France, Portugal, and Italy often greet colleagues they know by kissing both cheeks. Even people who know each other only a little may do this as a greeting.

Vocabulary

advice Ratschlag, Ratschläge
bow Verbeugung
immediately sofort
to kiss both cheeks beide Wangen küssen
to shake hands jdm. die Hand geben

Discuss with a partner which tips give good advice. Can you add any more tips?

Learning objectives
- Making visitors feel welcome
  Besuchern das Gefühl geben, willkommen zu sein
- Talking about travel options
  Reiseoptionen besprechen
- Explaining the schedule
  Den Ablauf erklären

2 Talking about plans

1 Work with a partner. Ask the questions below and make a note of the answers. Then tell the class what you found out.

1. Do you sometimes meet visitors when they arrive at the airport, at the station, or at your company?
2. How often are you the visitor? Does someone meet you?
3. Which countries do your visitors come from? Are they usually native or non-native speakers?

Vocabulary
company Firma
native speaker Muttersprachler/in

2 ◁08 Jonas is meeting Kim, an American visitor. Read and listen to the dialogue. What does Kim need to do?

a ☐ have a hot drink   c ☐ freshen up
b ☐ have a cold drink   d ☐ make a phone call

Vocabulary
absolutely freezing richtig kalt
actually tatsächlich
comfortable bequem
to freshen up sich frisch machen

Jonas   Kim, great to see you again!
Kim   Good to see you too, Jonas. How are you?
Jonas   I'm fine, thank you. Did you have a good trip?
Kim   Actually, it wasn't very comfortable. It was absolutely freezing on the train.
Jonas   Oh no. Do you need anything right now?
Kim   I'm OK for now, thanks.
Jonas   Can I get you something to drink? Water perhaps? Or a hot drink?
Kim   No, really. I'm fine. But is there a restroom somewhere?
Jonas   I'm sorry?
Kim   Is there somewhere I can freshen up?
Jonas   Oh sorry! Yes, of course, it's over there. I'll show you where it is.
Kim   Thanks, Jonas.

I'm sorry? / Sorry?
= I don't understand (can you say that again).
Oh sorry!
= I apologize (I didn't understand you).

Did you know?

In American English the word "toilet" is not polite, so use "restroom", "ladies' room", "men's room", or "bathroom". In British English the word "toilet" is fine.

3 Listen to the dialogue again and answer the questions.

1. How do you know that Kim and Jonas have met before?
2. Why was Kim's trip uncomfortable?
3. What does Jonas offer Kim?
4. Which question does Jonas not understand?

4 Look at the dialogue in exercise 2 again and complete the phrases below.

> **Phrases**
>
> **Offering something**
>
> Do ....¹ anything right now?
>
> Can ....² to drink?
>
> **Saying you want to freshen up**
>
> Is there ....³ somewhere?
>
> Is there somewhere I ....⁴?
> – Yes, of course, I'll show you where it is.

5 Match the questions to the answers and practice them with a partner.

1. Did you have a good flight?
2. Do you need anything right now?
3. Can I get you something to drink?
4. Is there a restroom somewhere?

a. Water would be great, thanks.
b. No, I'm OK for now, thanks.
c. Yes, it's over there.
d. Yes, it was fine, thank you.

6 🔊 09 Read and listen to these two dialogues. How do the visitors continue their journey?

a ☐ by train   b ☐ by car   c ☐ on foot

1

Ms. Evans	Sorry, my train was delayed. It's very nice of you to meet me here.
Mr. Ruiz	My pleasure. Can I help you with your bags, Ms. Evans?
Ms. Evans	No, I can manage, thanks.
Mr. Ruiz	My car's in the parking lot over there.
Ms. Evans	Where are we going from here?
Mr. Ruiz	Straight to the warehouse, if that's OK with you.
Ms. Evans	Sure. Is the warehouse far from here?
Mr. Ruiz	No, it takes about 15 minutes to get there.

> **Vocabulary**
>
> far weit
> it takes 15 minutes es dauert 15 Minuten
> parking lot Parkplatz
> straight direkt
> warehouse Lager

2

Akira	Would you like something to drink first?
Daniela	No, thanks. It was a long flight but I'm OK for now.
Akira	We can get a bus or a taxi from here.
Daniela	Where are we going first?
Akira	I'll take you to your hotel first, if that's all right with you.
Daniela	Great. I'd like to freshen up. Is the hotel far from here?
Akira	Not really. But you must be tired now. We can get a taxi.
Daniela	That would be great, thanks.

> It was a long <u>flight</u>. (not ~~a long fly~~)
>
> I'll <u>take</u> you to your hotel first. (not ~~I take you~~ ...)

Unit 2 . Talking about plans   13

7 Look at the dialogues in exercise 6 again and complete the phrases below.

> **Phrases**
>
> **Talking about travel options**
>
> My car's _____¹ over there.
>
> Where _____² from here?
>
> Is the warehouse _____³?
>
> We can _____⁴ from here.

8 Put the words into the correct order to make questions. Match the questions with the answers. Then work with a partner to ask and answer.

1 we | Where | are | going | first _____?

2 the | Is | far | here | from | office _____?

3 How | get | do | we | there _____?

4 there | Is | train | here | from | a _____?

a ▢ Yes, there is. There's a train in ten minutes.
b ▢ We can get a taxi from here. That's the easiest way to get there.
c ▢ Not really. It only takes ten minutes by bus, and there's a stop just over there.
d ▢ First I'll take you to your hotel, if that's OK.

9 ◀)) 10 Mrs. Schmidt and Mr. Todd are talking about their plans. Read and listen to the dialogue. Then complete Mr. Todd's diary.

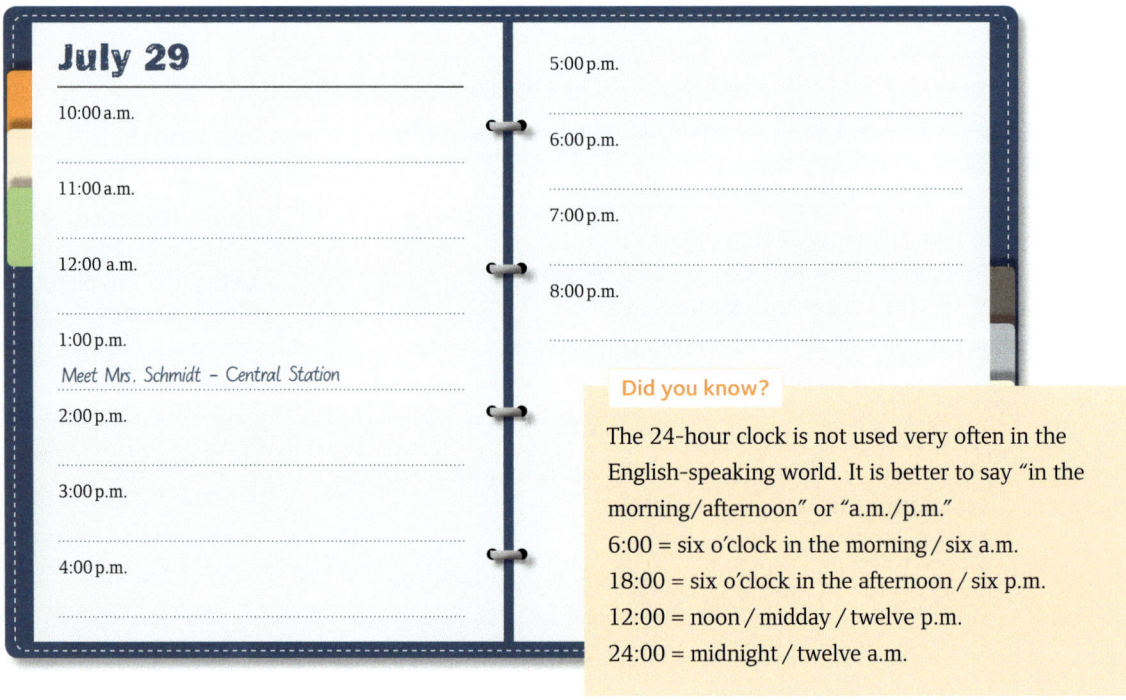

July 29

10:00 a.m.

11:00 a.m.

12:00 a.m.

1:00 p.m.
Meet Mrs. Schmidt – Central Station

2:00 p.m.

3:00 p.m.

4:00 p.m.

5:00 p.m.

6:00 p.m.

7:00 p.m.

8:00 p.m.

> **Did you know?**
>
> The 24-hour clock is not used very often in the English-speaking world. It is better to say "in the morning/afternoon" or "a.m./p.m."
> 6:00 = six o'clock in the morning / six a.m.
> 18:00 = six o'clock in the afternoon / six p.m.
> 12:00 = noon / midday / twelve p.m.
> 24:00 = midnight / twelve a.m.

Mr. Todd	My car's parked right outside. Can I help you with your luggage, Mrs. Schmidt?
Mrs. Schmidt	That's great, thanks.
Mr. Todd	Your train was on time. It's only ten after one. Would you like to check into your hotel before your meeting?
Mrs. Schmidt	Sure, thanks. Is the hotel far from here?
Mr. Todd	It's a ten-minute drive, so we can grab some lunch first.
Mrs. Schmidt	Sounds good.
Mr. Todd	You can go freshen up in your hotel after that.
Mrs. Schmidt	Thank you. When is my first appointment?
Mr. Todd	Your first meeting is at 3:00 p.m.
Mrs. Schmidt	Three o'clock, OK.
Mr. Todd	We're going to visit the showroom at four. And I'll pick you up for dinner at around 7:00 p.m. Is that OK for you?
Mrs. Schmidt	Could you pick me up a little later? I have some calls to make.
Mr. Todd	Sure, what time is good for you?
Mrs. Schmidt	Can we say 7:30?
Mr. Todd	Of course. I'll book a table for eight o'clock. I hope you like Italian food?
Mrs. Schmidt	Love it!

"Mrs." is used for married women. "Ms." is used for single women and if you don't know if a woman is married or not.

Vocabulary

appointment Termin
to grab some lunch Mittagessen gehen
on time pünktlich
to pick sb. up jdn. abholen
showroom Ausstellungsraum

10 Look at the dialogue in exercise 9 again and complete the phrases below.

Phrases

Explaining the schedule

Would you like to _____¹ your hotel before your meeting?

… we can grab _____² first.

You can go _____³ in your hotel after that.

_____⁴ is at 3:00 p.m.

We're going to _____⁵ at four.

And I'll _____⁶ for dinner at around 7:00 p.m.

Asking questions about the schedule

When is my _____⁷?

Could you pick me up _____⁸?

11 🔊 11 Dan and Maria are talking about the schedule and plans for the evening. Listen to their two conversations and answer the questions.

1 When is Maria's first appointment? a ☐ 10:00   b ☐ 10:30   c ☐ 11:00
2 What time will Dan book their table for? a ☐ 18:00   b ☐ 18:30   c ☐ 19:00

Key phrases

Here are some key phrases from the unit. Tick the ones that are useful for you.

Making visitors feel welcome
- Do you need anything right now?
- Can I get you something to drink?
- Would you like something to drink?

Saying you want to freshen up
- Is there a toilet (BE), a bathroom / ladies' room / men's room / restroom somewhere?
- Is there somewhere I can freshen up?

Explaining the schedule
- Would you like to check into your hotel before the meeting?
- I'll take you to your hotel.
- We can get/grab some lunch first.
- Your first meeting/appointment is at 3:00.
- We're going to visit the warehouse/showroom at 4:00.
- You can go freshen up in your hotel after that.
- I'll pick you up for dinner at around 7:00.
- Is that OK for you?
- What time is good for you?

Talking about plans

Talking about travel options
- My car / The parking lot / The bus stop is over there.
- Where are we going from here?
- We can get a taxi from here. That's the easiest way to get there.
- There's a train/bus in ten minutes.
- Is it / the hotel / the office far from here?

Asking questions about the schedule
- When is my first appointment?
- Could you pick me up a little later?

You will find an English–German list of these phrases on pages 60–61.

Use this space to write your own useful words and phrases.

Over to you

12 What phrases could you use when talking about your plans with a visitor? Write down how you would do the following.

Say where you would like to go: ....

Explain how you will get there: ....

Tell your visitor about lunch or dinner plans: ....

Now work with a partner and practice asking about plans and giving information. Then change roles and do the activity again. Partner A is the visitor, Partner B the host.

A Ask when the first appointment is.

B Reply and say what you'd like to do first.

A Reply and ask if you can go to your hotel first.

B Say yes. Offer lunch or dinner.

A Say if that's OK for you. Thank B.

Last but not least

13 Have a look at this online forum. Have you experienced something similar?

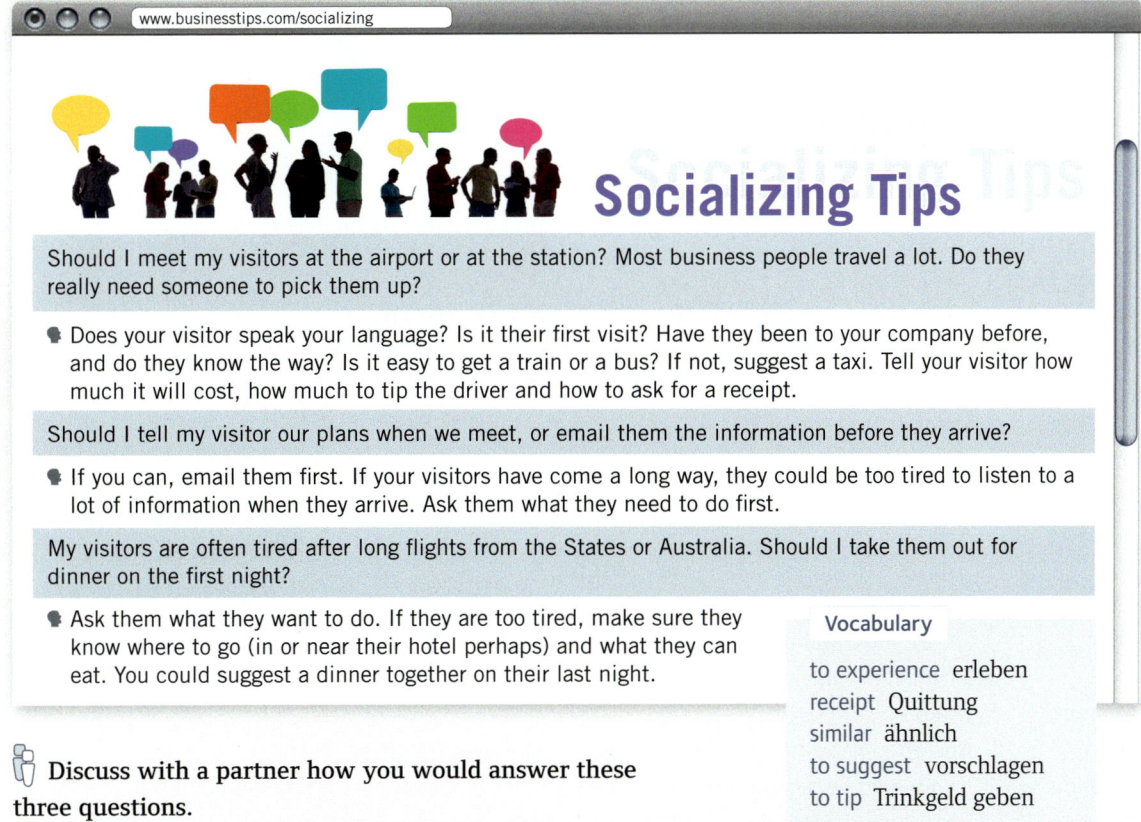

Socializing Tips

Should I meet my visitors at the airport or at the station? Most business people travel a lot. Do they really need someone to pick them up?

- Does your visitor speak your language? Is it their first visit? Have they been to your company before, and do they know the way? Is it easy to get a train or a bus? If not, suggest a taxi. Tell your visitor how much it will cost, how much to tip the driver and how to ask for a receipt.

Should I tell my visitor our plans when we meet, or email them the information before they arrive?

- If you can, email them first. If your visitors have come a long way, they could be too tired to listen to a lot of information when they arrive. Ask them what they need to do first.

My visitors are often tired after long flights from the States or Australia. Should I take them out for dinner on the first night?

- Ask them what they want to do. If they are too tired, make sure they know where to go (in or near their hotel perhaps) and what they can eat. You could suggest a dinner together on their last night.

Vocabulary

to experience erleben
receipt Quittung
similar ähnlich
to suggest vorschlagen
to tip Trinkgeld geben

Discuss with a partner how you would answer these three questions.

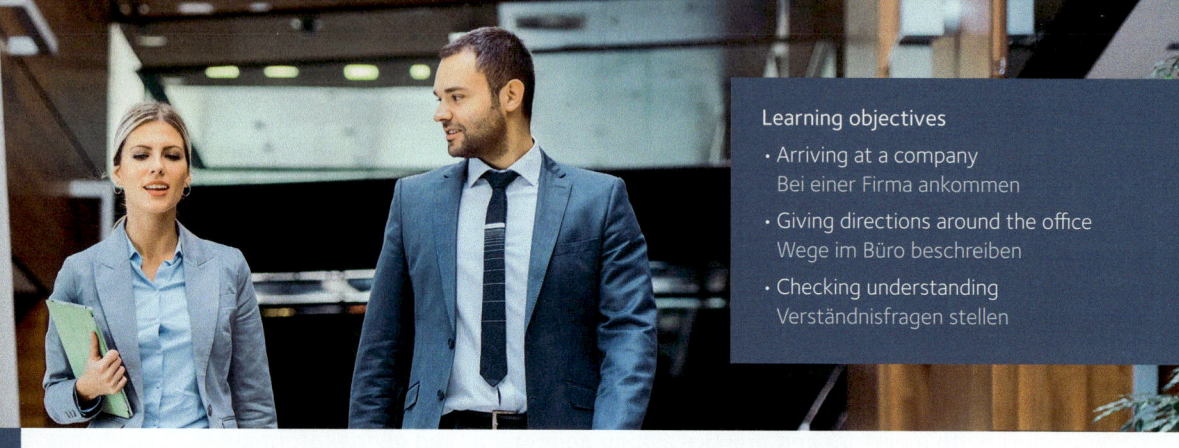

3 Welcoming a visitor to the company

Learning objectives
- Arriving at a company
  Bei einer Firma ankommen
- Giving directions around the office
  Wege im Büro beschreiben
- Checking understanding
  Verständnisfragen stellen

1 Work with a partner and talk about these questions.

1 Do you work for a company? Can you draw or describe your company logo?

2 Do you have visitor badges in your company? What information is on them?

Vocabulary

badge Ausweis
employee Mitarbeiter/in
valid until gültig bis

2 🔊 12 Read and listen to this dialogue. Who gives Amanda a visitor badge?

Receptionist	Good morning. Can I help you?
Amanda	Hello. My name's Amanda Howe. I'm here to see Theo Baltz.
Receptionist	Could you wait here a moment, please?
	I'll call him for you.
Amanda	Thank you.
…	
Theo	Amanda! Lovely to see you again.
Amanda	And you.
Theo	Welcome to SynTech. How was your trip?
Amanda	Fine, thanks.
Theo	I'll get you a visitor badge and then we can go to my office. You can leave your things there.
Amanda	Thanks.
Theo	And after we've had a coffee, I'll take you to meet the team.
Amanda	That would be nice, thanks.
Theo	Here's your badge. We can fill it out upstairs. Come this way, please.

I work at SynTech.
= Ich arbeite bei SynTech.
Welcome to SynTech.
= Willkommen bei SynTech.

18 English for Socializing and Small Talk

3 🔊 13 Amanda and Theo are in his office. Read and listen to the dialogue.
What does Amanda want to drink?

a ☐ Black coffee, no sugar
b ☐ White coffee, no sugar
c ☐ A cup of tea with no milk or sugar
d ☐ A cup of tea with milk

Theo	Can I take your jacket, Amanda?
Amanda	Ah yes, thanks. It's warm in here.
Theo	Would you like some coffee?
Amanda	I don't drink coffee, I'm afraid.
Theo	How about a cup of tea?
Amanda	That would be wonderful, thank you.
Theo	Here you are. Milk and sugar?
Amanda	Just milk, please. … Thanks.
Theo	You're welcome. And would you like a cookie?
Amanda	A cookie with my tea would be nice, thanks.
Theo	These are coconut.
Amanda	Perfect. Thank you very much.
Theo	Any time.

> Here you are.
> = Bitte. (wenn man jdm. etwas gibt/überreicht)
> You're welcome. / Not at all. / My pleasure. / Any time.
> = Bitte, gerne. Keine Ursache.

4 Look at the dialogues in exercises 2 and 3 again and complete the phrases below.

Phrases

Arriving at a company

Lovely ……………………………¹ again.
……………………………² SynTech.
I'll take you ……………………………³ the team.
Can I take ……………………………⁴, Amanda?
……………………………⁵ a cup of tea?
Here ……………………………⁶. Milk and sugar?
Thank you very much. – ……………………………⁷.

5 Put the words into the correct order to make questions.

1 wait | here | please | you | Could ……………………………?
2 I | take | Can | coat | your ……………………………?
3 tea | of | How about | cup | a ……………………………?
4 sugar | Do | and | take | you | milk ……………………………?

👥 Now match the questions to the answers and practice with a partner.

a ☐ Of course.
b ☐ Tea would be nice, thank you.
c ☐ A little milk, no sugar, thanks.
d ☐ Yes, thanks. And here's my scarf too.

6 🔊 14 Theo and Amanda are getting ready to go meet the team. Read and listen to the dialogue and look at the plan. Where does Amanda want to go first?

> **Vocabulary**
> conference room Besprechungsraum
> down the hallway am Ende des Flurs
> next to neben
> opposite gegenüber

Amanda   Where's the meeting this morning, Theo?
Theo   In room 742.
Amanda   Where's that?
Theo   It's on the seventh floor.
           We'll take the elevator.
           It's just down the hallway.
           Follow me.
Amanda   Can you tell me the way to the restroom first, please?
Theo   Of course. Go out of the door and turn right. It's the second door on the left. It's opposite the photocopier, next to the secretaries' office.
Amanda   Great, thanks.

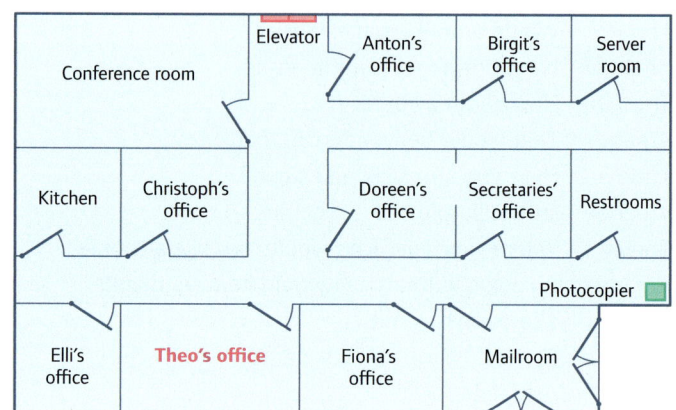

7 Look at the dialogue in exercise 6 again and complete the phrases below.

Phrases

Giving directions around the office

It's ………………¹ the seventh floor.

We'll take the elevator. It's ……………………………². Follow me.

Go out of the door and ……………………………³.

It's the second door ……………………………⁴.

It's opposite the photocopier, ……………………⁵ the secretaries' office.

Did you know?

When we are talking about the floors in a building, there is a difference between American and British English.
"Erdgeschoss"
= first floor (AE) –
   ground floor (BE)
"erste Etage"
= second floor (AE) –
   first floor (BE), etc.

8 Look at the plan again and complete the sentences with the correct word from the box.

> at • next to • on • on • opposite

1 The server room is ……………………… Birgit's office.
2 The conference room is the first door ……………………… the right.
3 The photocopier is ……………………… the end of the hallway.
4 The mailroom is ……………………… the second floor.
5 Theo's office is ……………………… Christoph's office.

English for Socializing and Small Talk

9 Work with a partner. Say where you are on the office plan, and ask your partner the way to a different place. When you get there, change roles.

A
I'm in the secretaries' office. Can you tell me the way to the kitchen, please?

B
Go out of the door and turn right. The kitchen's down the hallway on your right, opposite Elli's office.

10 ◁ 15 Amanda is chatting to her colleagues. Read and listen to three short dialogues. Does anyone talk about the weather?

1
Amanda   Hanif, are you still working with Mr. Jaffrey in the Lahore office?
Hanif   Sorry, could you say that again?
Amanda   You work in Lahore, right? With Mr. Jaffrey?
Hanif   Ah, you mean Salim Jaffrey? Yes, that's right. A very nice man.

2
Amanda   I think we should take ten.
Theo   Sorry, I don't quite understand …
Amanda   I mean, take a ten-minute break. It's stuffy in here.
Theo   What do you mean by "stuffy" – no fresh air? OK, I'll open some windows.

3
Theo   Can we contact Harry in London, Amanda?
Amanda   No, sorry. He's still a bit under the weather.
Theo   The weather? Could you explain what you mean?
Amanda   Oh, I mean he's not very well. He's not in the office this week.

Vocabulary
to be under the weather   angeschlagen sein
fresh air frische Luft
stuffy stickig
to take a break / take ten   eine (kurze) Pause machen

a <u>ten-minute</u> break
(not ~~a ten minutes break~~)

11 Look at the dialogues in exercise 10 again and complete the phrases below.

Phrases

Checking understanding

Sorry, could you ....¹?

Ah, ...² Salim Jaffrey?

Sorry, I ....³.

What ....⁴ "stuffy" – no fresh air?

Could you explain ....⁵?

12 Match the questions (1–5) with the answers (a–e). Then practice with a partner.

1 What do you mean by "accommodation"?
2 What does "expand" mean?
3 Let's call it a day. – Sorry, I don't quite understand.
4 It's chilly. – What do you mean by "chilly"?
5 A green thumb? Could you explain what you mean?

a It's not very warm in here.
b I mean, let's stop now.
c It's a place to stay.
d Good at gardening.
e It means to get bigger.

Unit 3 . Welcoming a visitor to the company   21

Key phrases

Here are some key phrases from the unit. Tick the ones that are useful for you.

Arriving at a company
- Lovely to see you again.
- Welcome to …
- I'll get you a visitor badge.
- You can leave your things in my office.
- Can I take your jacket/coat?
- Would you like a coffee?
- How about a cup of tea?
- I'll take you to meet the team.
- Come this way. / Follow me.
- Thank you very much. – You're welcome. / Not at all. / My pleasure. / Any time.

Giving directions around the office
- The conference room is on the seventh floor.
- We'll take the elevator (AE) / lift (BE).
- It's just down the hallway (AE) / corridor (BE).
- It's the first/second door on the left/right.
- It's opposite / next to the mailroom.
- Come with me, I'll show you.

Welcoming a visitor to the company

Checking understanding
- Sorry, could you say that again?
- Do you mean …?
- Sorry, I don't quite understand.
- What do you mean (by …)?
- Could you explain what you mean?

You will find an English–German list of these phrases on pages 61–62.

Use this space to write your own useful words and phrases.

....

....

....

....

....

....

....

....

Over to you

13 Think of a situation when you have a visitor at work. Where do you meet your visitor? Do you usually show visitors around the office? Write down how you would do the following.

Welcome a visitor who has just arrived: ....

Offer your visitor something to drink: ....

Explain where the restroom is: ....

Work with a partner and practice the dialogue. Then change roles and do the activity again. Partner A is the host, Partner B the visitor.

A Welcome a visitor at reception.

B Reply.

A Take B to your office and offer to take his/her coat.

B Reply.

A Offer your visitor a drink.

B Thank A and say what you'd like to drink.

B Ask the way to the restroom.

A Tell B the way.

Last but not least

14 Understanding people with foreign accents can be difficult. Read the exchange below. Do you sometimes have the same problem understanding foreign accents?

www.forum.com

Understanding foreign accents

English is not my first language, but I have little or no problem understanding native speakers. I work mostly with colleagues from the States and some of them speak fast but very clearly. I can understand British people, but not if they speak in a strong regional dialect. I find some non-native speakers very hard to understand when they speak English. It's embarrassing if I have to ask them to repeat what they say. Any tips?

- Don't worry if you don't understand. Say sorry and ask the other person to repeat what they said.
- Repeat the words you don't understand and ask if that's right.
- Ask the speaker to speak more slowly.
- If you're on the phone, ask for an email.
- Just smile as if you can understand.
- Ask the speaker to spell the word or name you can't understand.

Vocabulary

as if als ob
embarrassing peinlich
foreign ausländisch

Discuss these questions with a partner.
Which accents do you find hard to understand?
What do you do when you can't understand?
Which tips are the best, do you think?

Learning objectives
- Introducing colleagues
  Kollegen vorstellen
- Talking about people you both know
  Über gemeinsame Kontakte reden
- Talking about where you are from
  Darüber sprechen, wo man herkommt

4 Chatting with colleagues

1 When you welcome a new colleague to your company, how important is it to …

		very important	not important
1	be at reception when the new colleague arrives?	☐	☐
2	introduce your colleague to the team?	☐	☐
3	show him/her where the restrooms are?	☐	☐
4	offer your new colleague something to drink?	☐	☐
5	talk about where he/she is from?	☐	☐
6	talk about people you both know?	☐	☐

Now discuss your answers with a partner.

2 🔊 16 Mia from HR is introducing Linda, who is new to the Zurich office, to her colleagues. Read and listen to the dialogues. Who has Linda had contact with before?

1
Mia	Can I get you a coffee, Linda? Or some water?
Linda	No, I'm fine, thanks. But perhaps you can show me where the toilets are.
Mia	Of course, just follow me.
Paolo	Hi, Mia.
Mia	Hi, Paolo. I'd like to introduce a new colleague. This is Linda. Linda has come to work with us from our London office. She's in R&D. Linda, this is Paolo from the sales department.
Paolo	It's a pleasure to meet you.
Linda	And you.

Vocabulary

HR (human resources) Personalabteilung
R&D (research and development)
   Forschung und Entwicklung
sales department Vertriebsabteilung

2
Mia	Kim, have you met Linda yet?
Kim	No, not yet. But we've had a lot of email contact. Good to meet you at last, Linda.
Linda	And you. It's nice to put a face to the name! How are you?
Kim	I'm good, thanks. And you? Did you find us OK?
Linda	Yes, no problem, thanks.

English for Socializing and Small Talk

3

Mia	Linda, this is Nick. Have you two met before?
Nick	Yes, we have. I think we met in Berlin last year.
Linda	That's right. It's good to see you again. You're in IT, aren't you?
Nick	No, actually I work in HR with Mia.
Linda	Oh, yes. So, how are things?
Nick	Good, thanks. And with you?

> **Did you know?**
>
> When someone asks "How are you?", the answers "I'm good" or "I'm fine/well" are both correct: "I'm good" is more informal. The more formal "How do you do?" when you are introduced to someone is not a real question, and you answer it with "How do you do?"

3 Look at the three dialogues in exercise 2 again and complete the phrases below.

> **Phrases**
>
> **Introducing colleagues**
>
> I'd like to introduce _____ [1].
>
> _____ [2] Linda. … She's in R&D.
>
> Kim, _____ [3] yet? – No, not yet.
>
> Have you two _____ [4]? – Yes, we have.
>
> It's good _____ [5].
>
> **Welcoming a new colleague**
>
> It's a pleasure _____ [6]. – And you.
>
> Good to meet you at last. – And you. It's nice _____ [7] to the name!
>
> How are you? – I'm _____ [8].
>
> How are things? – Good, thanks. And _____ [9]?

4 Match the parts of these sentences.

1	I'd like to	a	aren't you?
2	This is	b	in the sales department.
3	John works	c	Peter, a new project manager in IT.
4	Have you	d	introduce you to Linda.
5	You're in sales,	e	met Sarah before?

5 🔊 17 **Read and listen to Mia and Linda talking about people they know. Who do they talk about?**

Mia	How's Tanya these days?
Linda	She's fine. We spoke on the phone last week.
Mia	Does she still work at the London office?
Linda	Yes, she does. She's doing really well.
Mia	Say hello from me next time you speak.
Linda	Sure. How about Joe? Is he still with the company?
Mia	Joe Baker? He's not, no. He left last month.
Linda	What's he doing now?
Mia	He works in Basel.
Linda	Are you still in touch with him?
Mia	Yes, we keep in touch. Well, we write emails. We don't often speak.

Vocabulary

to be in touch with sb.
  mit jdm. in Kontakt sein
to keep in touch
  in Verbindung bleiben

6 Look at the dialogue in exercise 5 again and complete the phrases below.

Phrases

Talking about people you both know

How's Tanya ....¹?

............................² at the London office?

............................³ Joe? Is he still ....⁴?

............................⁵ now?

Are you still ....⁶ with him?

7 Complete the sentences below with the correct word from the box.

at • in • on • with • with

1 We spoke .... the phone last week.

2 Is Peter still .... the Dublin office?

3 Is Angela still .... the company?

4 She's working .... Berlin.

5 Are you in touch .... him?

8 🔊 18 **Listen to Linda and Nick talking about Joe. What kind of company does Joe work for?**

Listen to the dialogue again and tick what you hear.

1 a ☐ Does he still work in sales?
  b ☐ Is he still in sales?

2 a ☐ He was good at his job too.
  b ☐ He had a good job too.

3 a ☐ Are you still in touch with him?
  b ☐ Do you keep in touch?

4 a ☐ I'm sorry to hear that.
  b ☐ I'm very sorry about that.

9 🔊 19 Mary and Debbie are having lunch in the company canteen. Read and listen to the dialogue. Which sentence is correct – a or b?

 a Hans was born in Vienna but he lives in Leipzig now.
 b Debbie was born in Boston but she lives in Leipzig now.

Mary	So how are you getting on, Debbie?
Debbie	Fine, thanks. I …
Hans	Do you mind if I join you?
Mary	Not at all. Hans, have you met Debbie?
Hans	No, not yet. Hans Seidel, pleased to meet you.
Debbie	And you. Which department are you in, Hans?
Hans	I'm in sales, but I don't work in Leipzig now. I'm just here for meetings.
Debbie	So … where do you work?
Hans	In Vienna.
Debbie	Beautiful city. Where are you from originally?
Hans	I was born here in Leipzig, but I moved to Austria a few years ago. What about you?
Debbie	I'm from the States … from Boston …
Hans	Ah yes, that's a beautiful city too.
Debbie	Have you been to Boston?
Hans	Actually, no, but I'd love to go there. Do you miss America?
Debbie	No, I'm very happy here. I like living in Leipzig.

Vocabulary

canteen Kantine
Do you mind if I join you?
    Darf ich mich dazu setzen?
How are you getting on?
    Wie kommen Sie zurecht?
originally ursprünglich

Do you know any of the three cities which Hans and Debbie talk about? Discuss them in class.

10 Look at the dialogue in exercise 9 again and complete the phrases below.

> **Phrases**
>
> **Talking about where you are from**
>
> .... ¹ originally?
>
> .... ² here in Leipzig, but I moved to Austria a few years ago.
>
> .... ³ the States.
>
> .... ⁴ America?

11 Match the questions with the answers.

1 Have you two met yet?
2 Which department are you in?
3 Where do you work?
4 Where are you from originally?
5 Do you miss Switzerland?
6 Have you been to Barcelona?

a I'm from the States.
b No, but I'd like to go there.
c I'm in R&D.
d No, I'm very happy here.
e No, not yet, but we've had email contact.
f I usually work at the Basel office.

Key phrases

Here are some key phrases from the unit. Tick the ones that are useful for you.

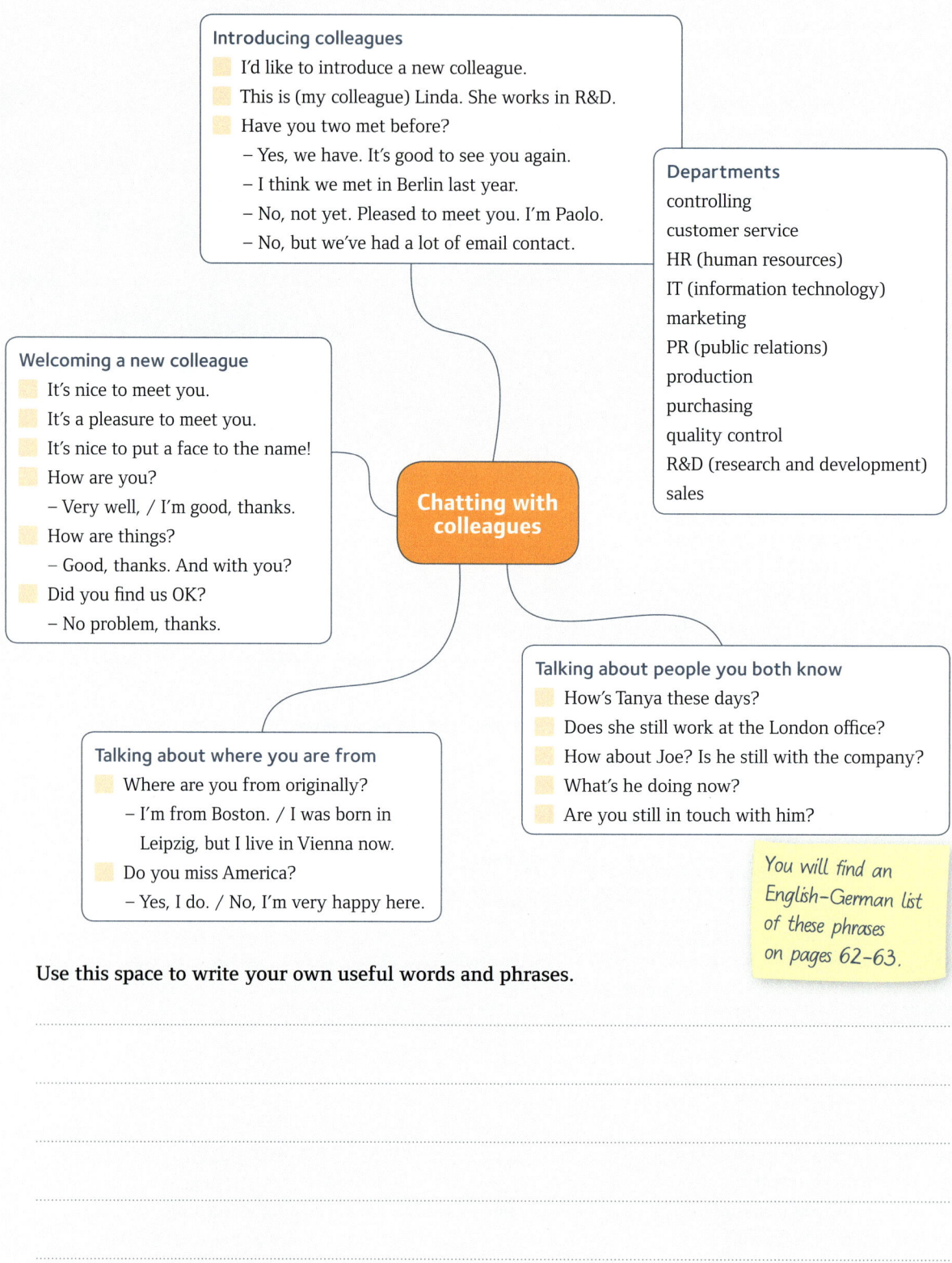

Introducing colleagues
- I'd like to introduce a new colleague.
- This is (my colleague) Linda. She works in R&D.
- Have you two met before?
  – Yes, we have. It's good to see you again.
  – I think we met in Berlin last year.
  – No, not yet. Pleased to meet you. I'm Paolo.
  – No, but we've had a lot of email contact.

Departments
controlling
customer service
HR (human resources)
IT (information technology)
marketing
PR (public relations)
production
purchasing
quality control
R&D (research and development)
sales

Welcoming a new colleague
- It's nice to meet you.
- It's a pleasure to meet you.
- It's nice to put a face to the name!
- How are you?
  – Very well, / I'm good, thanks.
- How are things?
  – Good, thanks. And with you?
- Did you find us OK?
  – No problem, thanks.

Chatting with colleagues

Talking about people you both know
- How's Tanya these days?
- Does she still work at the London office?
- How about Joe? Is he still with the company?
- What's he doing now?
- Are you still in touch with him?

Talking about where you are from
- Where are you from originally?
  – I'm from Boston. / I was born in Leipzig, but I live in Vienna now.
- Do you miss America?
  – Yes, I do. / No, I'm very happy here.

You will find an English–German list of these phrases on pages 62–63.

Use this space to write your own useful words and phrases.

....

....

....

....

Over to you

12 Think of a situation where you welcome a new colleague to your company. Write down how you would do the following.

Make your new colleague feel welcome:
....

Introduce the new colleague to the team:
....

Ask where you new colleague is from and where he/she lives and works now:
....
....

Now work with two partners and practice the dialogue. Then change roles and do the activity again. Partner A and Partner C are talking to Partner B, a new colleague.

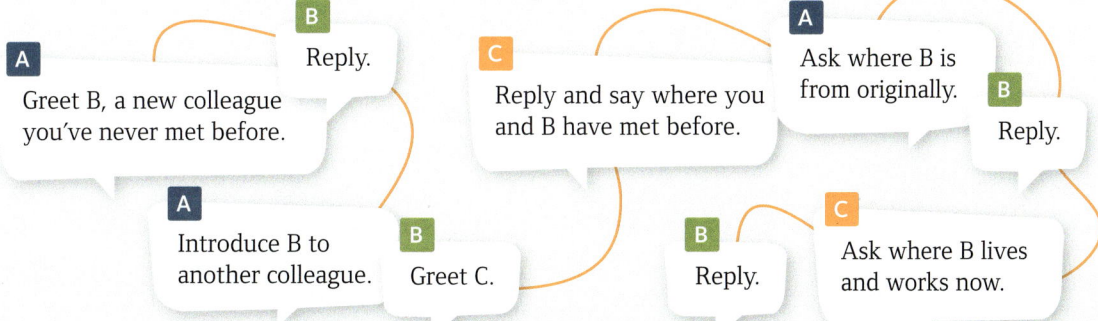

Last but not least

13 Read this blog post. Do you agree with the advice?

Vocabulary

to be comfortable sich wohlfühlen
cell phone Handy
to exchange austauschen
to focus on sich konzentrieren auf
to keep the conversation going
　　das Gespräch am Laufen halten

How to start small talk … and keep it going

>> It's important to make small talk with your colleagues. You don't have to be best friends, but you want the other person to be comfortable talking to you. Don't look around at other people in the room or at your cell phone – focus on the person you're with.

>> Show them you're interested in them by asking questions: "Tell me more about your work." or "Where are you from originally?"

>> Questions like "Do you like living here?" might get a one-word answer, so if the other person just says Yes or No, ask another question: "So what do/don't you like about it?" And tell them something about yourself to keep the conversation going: "I've lived here for over ten years and I'm really happy here."

How do you keep a conversation going? Exchange tips with a partner.

Learning objectives

- Talking about sightseeing
  Über Sehenswürdigkeiten reden
- Asking for / giving directions
  Wegbeschreibungen erfragen/geben
- Inviting and responding to invitations
  Einladen und auf Einladungen reagieren

5 Entertaining a visitor

1 Work with a partner. Look at the leaflet below. Where would you take a visitor that you were entertaining? What can you add to the leaflet?

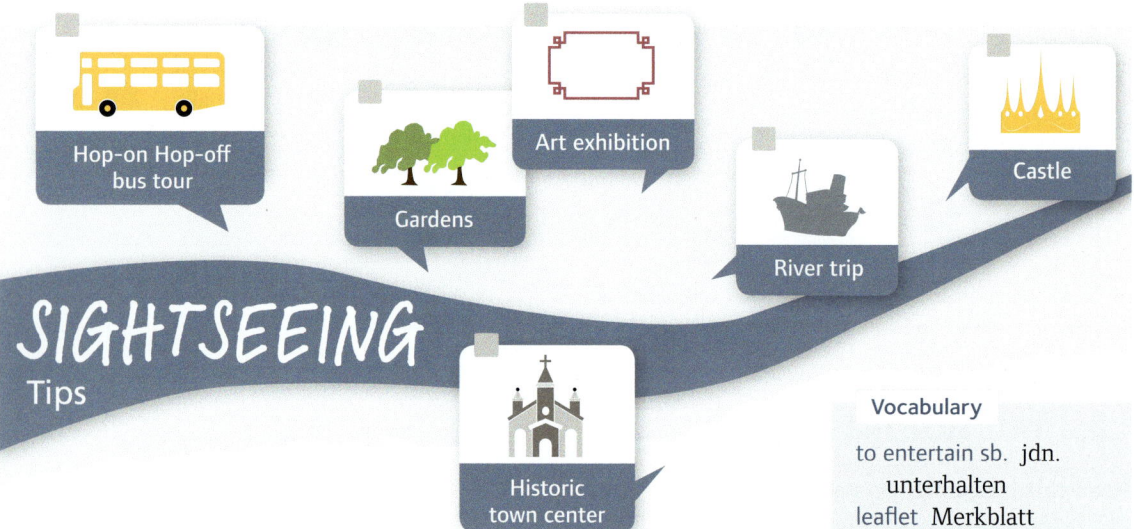

Vocabulary

to entertain sb. jdn. unterhalten
leaflet Merkblatt

2 ◁ 20 Anton is entertaining Beth, a visitor to his company. Put their conversation into the correct order. Then listen and check.

a I'll be happy to show you around the city then.

b It's been a long day. How are you doing, Beth?

c Thank you, Anton.

d I know, but don't worry. I'm free to do some sightseeing tomorrow.

e Fine thanks, but I have been very busy.

f I'm afraid you have one more appointment today.

You have one more appointment. (not one more date)

1 *b* 2 ☐ 3 ☐ 4 ☐ 5 ☐ 6 ☐

30 English for Socializing and Small Talk

3 🔊21 Anton has picked Beth up from her hotel. Read and listen to the dialogue. Anton suggests something that is not on the leaflet in exercise 1. What is it?

Anton   Is this your first time in Heidelberg?
Beth   No, I was here last winter, but it was very cold, too cold for sightseeing.
Anton   Oh well, it's lovely weather now. We could take a boat trip on the river.
Beth   That sounds nice. Do you have any more tips for things to do?
Anton   There's a very interesting castle. You should see that. I can take you there.
Beth   I'd love to see that, thank you. I'm interested in historic buildings.
Anton   Then perhaps you should see our famous church in the market place too. We can go there first if you like.
Beth   That's a good idea. I'd like that very much.

Beth is interested in historic buildings.
(the person is interested in something)

The castle is interesting to visit.
(the place is interesting)

4 Listen to the dialogue again and answer the questions.

1 Has Beth been to Germany before?
2 Why didn't she go sightseeing last winter?
3 Why would Beth love to see the castle?

5 Look at the dialogue in exercise 3 again and complete the phrases below.

┌─ Phrases
│
│ **Talking about sightseeing tips**
│
│ ....¹ a boat trip on the river.
│
│ That ....².
│
│ Do you have ....³ for things to do?
│
│ There's ....⁴. You should see that.
│
│ ....⁵ see that, thank you.
│
│ ....⁶ historic buildings.
│
│ We can go there first ....⁷.
│
│ That's a ....⁸.
│
│ ....⁹ very much.

6 Match the sentences with the responses and practice them with a partner.

1 I'd love to see the castle.   a That's a good idea.
2 Do you have any sightseeing tips?   b I'd like that very much, thank you.
3 You could take a boat trip.   c You should see the old castle then.
4 I can take you there if you like.   d I can take you there if you like.
5 I'm interested in historic buildings.   e Oh yes, there are lots of things to do.

Unit 5 . Entertaining a visitor   31

7 🔊22 Anya, a visitor, is asking for directions. Read and listen to the dialogues. Where is she?

Dialogue 1: ☐ cafe ☐ bistro   Dialogue 2: ☐ drugstore ☐ book store

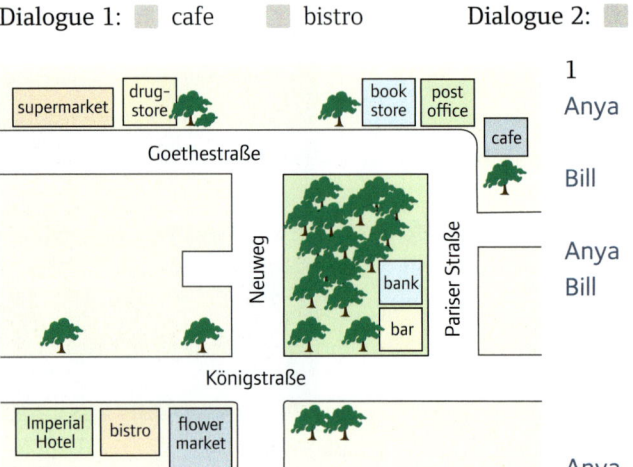

1

Anya	Bill, I want to do some shopping. Can you tell me where the nearest ATM is?
Bill	Sure, there's a bank on Pariser Straße. You'll find an ATM there.
Anya	How do I get there from here?
Bill	Go along here and take the second street on your left. There's a bar on the corner of Königstraße and Pariser Straße, and the bank is on your left next to the bar. It's near a big park, you can't miss it.
Anya	Thank you.

2

Anya	Excuse me! I'm lost. How do I get to the Imperial Hotel from here?
Man	Go along Goethestraße and take the first street on your right. When you come to Königstraße, turn right again and you'll see the hotel on your left.
Anya	Is it far?
Man	No, about ten minutes.
Anya	Great, thank you very much.

> **Vocabulary**
> ATM Geldautomat
> I'm lost. Ich habe mich verlaufen.
> Is it far? Ist es weit?
> to turn left/right links/rechts abbiegen
> You can't miss it. Sie können es nicht übersehen.

> on your <u>left/right</u>
> (not ~~on your left/right side~~)
> <u>near</u> the park
> (not ~~in the near of~~)

8 Look at the dialogues in exercise 7 again and complete the phrases below.

> **Phrases**
>
> **Asking for directions**
>
> .... ¹ where the nearest ATM is?
>
> How .... ² from here?
>
> Excuse me! .... ³. How do I get to the Imperial Hotel from here?
>
> .... ⁴? – No, about ten minutes.
>
> **Giving directions**
>
> There's a bar .... ⁵ Königstraße and Pariser Straße.
>
> The bank is .... ⁶ next to the bar.
>
> .... ⁷ Goethestraße and .... ⁸ on your right.
>
> .... ⁹ right again and .... ¹⁰ the hotel on your left.

9 👥 Work with a partner. Look at the map, say where you are, and ask the way to different places.

> I'm in the supermarket. Where can I get a cup of coffee?

10 🔊23 Read and listen to colleagues discussing plans. Who is having dinner together?

1
Elisa   Brenda Rice is visiting from L.A. How about meeting for lunch today?
Ken   I'd love to, but I'm afraid I don't have time.
Elisa   Maybe we could meet after work instead. Fritz and I are planning to take Brenda out for dinner. Would you like to join us?
Ken   I'm sorry but I'm busy tonight. Perhaps I could meet you tomorrow. What about lunch?
Elisa   Yes, we could have lunch in the canteen at twelve.
Ken   I'd like to do that, thanks.

2
Elisa   Do you have any plans for this evening?
Brenda No, but I have an early meeting tomorrow …
Elisa   Ah well, we would like to take you out for dinner. Perhaps an early dinner?
Brenda That's very kind of you. I'd love to try some traditional German food.
Elisa   OK, we can take you for some *Maultaschen*. It's a local specialty.
Brenda That sounds very nice. Thank you.

> **Vocabulary**
> instead stattdessen
> to join sb. jdm. Gesellschaft leisten

11 Listen to the dialogue again and answer the questions.
1 Why can't Ken have dinner with his colleagues?
2 Find two ways that Ken refuses Elisa's invitations.
3 How does Brenda accept the invitation?

12 Look at the dialogues in exercise 10 again and complete the phrases below.

> **Phrases**
>
> **Inviting**
>
> How about _____¹ today?
>
> Would you like _____²?
>
> We would like _____³ for dinner.
>
> **Responding to invitations**
>
> I'd love to, but I'm afraid _____⁴.
>
> _____⁵ I'm busy tonight.
>
> Perhaps I could _____⁶.
>
> _____⁷ of you.
>
> _____⁸ very nice. Thank you.

13 Replace the phrases in *italics* with phrases from the dialogue that mean the same thing.
1 *Would you like to meet* for lunch today?
2 *I'm sorry* I don't have time.
3 Would you like to *come with us*?
4 *I don't have time* tonight.
5 *Are you doing anything* this evening?
6 That's *really nice* of you.

Unit 5 . Entertaining a visitor

Key phrases

Here are some key phrases from the unit. Tick the ones that are useful for you.

Asking for sightseeing tips
- ☐ Do you have any tips for things to do?
- ☐ I'd love to see that, thank you.
- ☐ That's a good idea. I'd like to do that.

Giving sightseeing tips
- ☐ There's an interesting museum.
- ☐ You could take a boat trip on the river.
- ☐ I can take you there if you like.

Asking for directions
- ☐ Where is the nearest ATM?
- ☐ Excuse me, can you tell me where the bank is?
- ☐ I'm lost. How do I get to the Imperial Hotel from here?
- ☐ Is it far?

Giving directions
- ☐ It's opposite the park near the cafe.
- ☐ It's next to the hotel.
- ☐ Go along this street, then turn left/right.
- ☐ Take the first/second/third street on your left/right.
- ☐ You can walk from here.

Entertaining a visitor

Inviting
- ☐ How about meeting for lunch tomorrow?
- ☐ Would you like to join us for dinner later?
- ☐ We would like to take you out for dinner.

Accepting or refusing invitations
- ☐ That sounds very nice. Thank you.
- ☐ Thanks, I'd like to do that.
- ☐ That's very kind of you. I'd love to.
- ☐ I'd love to, but I'm afraid I don't have time.
- ☐ I'm sorry but I'm busy later. How about tomorrow?
- ☐ Maybe we could meet for dinner instead?

You will find an English–German list of these phrases on pages 63–64.

Use this space to write your own useful words and phrases.

....
....
....
....
....
....
....

Over to you

14 Think of a situation where you have to give directions. Write down how you would do the following.

Tell someone about a popular tourist attraction:

....

Say how far the attraction is from your company and how to get there:

....

> **Vocabulary**
>
> to direct sb. somewhere
> jdn. irgendwohin leiten
> popular beliebt, berühmt

Now work with a partner, decide on a place to start from and practice the dialogue. Then change roles and do the activity again. Partner A is the visitor, Partner B the host.

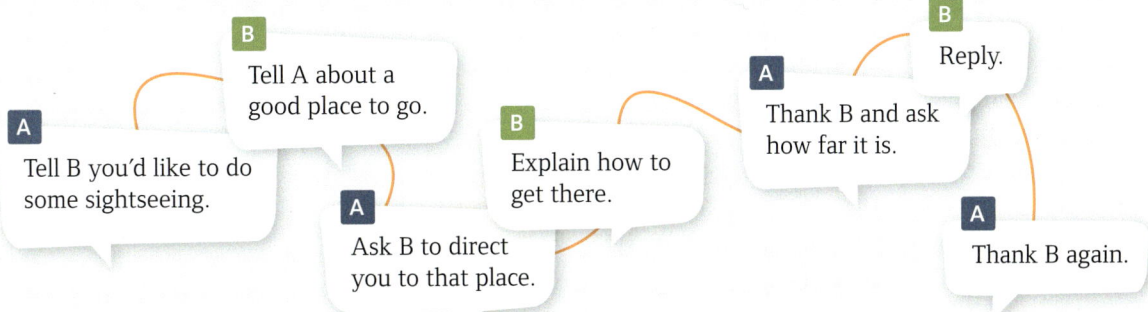

Last but not least

15 Read about entertaining business partners. Is this something you have to do for your work?

Entertaining a business partner …

… can be tricky if you don't know that person very well. So, take the first opportunity when you're making small talk to find out what they like doing. What are their free-time interests? Can you match their interests with an invitation?
What could you offer these three business partners? Would you invite them to do something with you, or suggest something they can do alone?

Jonny is from Australia. He arrived this morning and has been in meetings all day. You know his wife is a singer and that he's very interested in music. What could you offer Jonny?

Geert is a big football fan from Holland, and he's working on a project with you this month. He's in a company apartment with a very small kitchen. What could you suggest to Geert?

Irena is Polish, rather shy. She has meetings at your company on Friday and Monday, so she will be alone on the weekend. You know she's interested in historic buildings and art. Do you have any sightseeing ideas for Irena?

> **Vocabulary**
>
> to match zuordnen
> opportunity Gelegenheit
> shy schüchtern
> tricky schwierig

What would you do with these visitors? Exchange ideas with a partner.

6 Eating out

1 Work with a partner and discuss where you would take these visitors for a meal.

- An important client from India
- A group of young American interns
- A colleague you know well from the U.K.
- An international group of government officials

> **Vocabulary**
>
> government official Regierungsbeamter/ Regierungsbeamtin
> intern Praktikant/in

How often do you take visitors out to dinner?
Where do you take them and why?

2 ◁) 24 Karl has two visitors in the office today, and he would like to take them out to dinner. Read and listen to the dialogue. Who eats fish?

Karl	Let's call it a day and get something to eat. How hungry are you?
Omar	Well, we had a big lunch, but I am quite hungry again now.
Karl	Good, because I'm starving! What kind of food do you like?
Sally	We're new here. What do you recommend?
Karl	It depends. Are you vegetarian?
Omar	Yes, I don't eat meat or fish.
Sally	I eat fish but I can't eat seafood. I'm allergic to it.
Karl	I love seafood, but I don't often eat it. OK, not the Brunnenkeller then. They don't have many vegetarian dishes. Do you like Indian food?
Sally	No, I'm afraid I don't really care for it.
Karl	What about Thai food?
Sally	I'm not sure.
Omar	Will they have a vegetarian option?
Karl	Yes, probably. It's very spicy.
Sally	I'm sorry, I don't like spicy food.
Karl	Do you like Italian food?
Sally	Oh yes, I prefer Italian to Thai food.
Karl	Well I can recommend Marco's. They don't have a big menu, but the food is very good.
Omar	Sounds great!

! menu = Speisekarte
set meal = Menü

> **Vocabulary**
>
> to be allergic to sth. gegen etw. allergisch sein
> I don't care for it. Ich mag es nicht sonderlich.
> I'm starving! Ich sterbe vor Hunger!
> It depends. Es kommt darauf an.
> to recommend sth. etw. empfehlen
> seafood Meeresfrüchte
> spicy scharf, würzig

3 Match the sentences that mean the same thing.

1 I'm vegetarian.
2 I don't care much for seafood.
3 I prefer fish to meat.
4 I can recommend the fish.
5 I'm allergic to seafood.

a I like fish better than meat.
b The fish here is very good.
c I can't eat seafood.
d I don't like seafood much.
e I don't eat meat or fish.

4 Look at the dialogue in exercise 2 again and complete the phrases below.

> **Phrases**
>
> **Talking about what to eat**
>
> How hungry ....¹?
>
> ....² do you like? – We're new here. What ....³?
>
> Are you ....⁴? – Yes, I don't eat meat or fish.
>
> I eat fish but I can't eat seafood. ....⁵ to it.
>
> ....⁶ Indian food? – No, I'm afraid ....⁷.
>
> Will they have ....⁸? – Yes, probably.
>
> ....⁹ Italian to Thai food.

5 Match the parts to make complete sentences.

1 I love seafood
2 I would prefer Italian food
3 I can recommend Marco's
4 I only had a small lunch
5 I can't eat nuts

because
but
so

it's not too spicy.
I'm allergic to them.
I don't often eat it.
I'm starving now.
the food is good.

6 Sort the words into the correct categories in the table.

~~appetizer~~ · ~~beef~~ · cabbage · chicken · delicious · dessert · French fries · lamb · main course · onion · pepper · pork · potato · rice · salad · savory · spicy · sweet

Parts of a meal	Types of meat	Types of vegetable	Side dishes	Words for describing food
appetizer	beef			

Add any words you know to the lists. Work with a partner and say what you (don't) like.

7 🔊 25 Karl and Louise are in a restaurant. Read and listen to the dialogue. What does Louise choose?

Louise   Hmm, it's a long time since lunch. I'm starving!
Karl   Well, that's good because the portions are big here. Can I help you with the menu?
Louise   Yes, please. So what's *Pfifferlinge in Rahm*? Is that a type of meat?
Karl   No, it's actually a type of mushroom. It's a specialty of our region. And *Rahm* means cream, so it's made with cream. It's delicious. You should try it.
Louise   Sounds good. I'll have that.
Karl   Do you know what you would like for your main course?
Louise   *Schwein* is pork, right? Hmmm, not my favorite meat. But it comes with French fries. And what's *Hirschbraten*?
Karl   *Hirsch* is deer … but I think you call the meat of the deer … um …
Louise   Oh yeah, venison. And it comes with … *Spätzle*? Is that potato?
Karl   No, it's more like pasta. They're good here, but not as good as my mother makes! Ah, here's the waiter. Are you ready to order?
Louise   Yes, I'll have the mushrooms as an appetizer. And the venison, well-done, please.
Karl   Good choice! And I'd like the vegetable soup and the pork. I love French fries!

> Can I help you with the <u>menu</u>?
> (not: ~~Can I help you with the card?~~)
> I<u>'ll have</u> the mushrooms.
> (not ~~I have the mushrooms.~~)

Vocabulary

choice Wahl
to try probieren
well-done durchgegart, durchgebraten

Did you know?

When you raise your glass, you say "Cheers!" and before you begin to eat, you can say "Enjoy your meal". Some English speakers use the French expression "Bon appetit".

8 Look at the dialogue in exercise 7 again and complete the phrases below.

Phrases

Helping with the menu

Can I help you _____¹?

So what's *Pfifferlinge in Rahm*? Is that _____² meat?

_____³ of our region. … It's _____⁴ cream.

It's delicious. You should _____⁵.

The pork comes with French fries.

Ordering a meal

Do you know what you would like _____⁶?

Are you ready _____⁷?

Yes, _____⁸ the mushrooms _____⁹.

And _____¹⁰ the vegetable soup and the pork.

9 Put the sentences in the correct order and practice the dialogue with a partner.

- ☐ It's a type of pasta made with cheese.
- ☐ And do you know what you want as an appetizer?
- ☐ I'll have that as my main course. It sounds good.
- ☐ 1 Can I help you with the menu?
- ☐ Yes, I'll have the tomato soup.
- ☐ Yes, please. What's *Kasespätzle*?

10 ◁)26 Karl and Louise have finished their meal. Read and listen to the dialogue. Who pays for the meal, and why?

Louise	I'm full. I ate too much, but it was delicious. Thank you.
Karl	How about a dessert?
Louise	Oh, no thank you. I've had enough to eat.
Karl	OK, should I get the check?
Louise	Yes, please. Good idea.
Karl	Excuse me! Can we get the check, please?
Louise	Hey, let me get this.
Karl	No, that's all right. I'll pay for it.
Louise	Seriously, this is on me. You're helping me so much with the new project. I want to thank you.
Karl	Are you sure? That's very kind of you.
Louise	Don't mention it. Do they take credit cards here?
Karl	Yes, they do.
Louise	And do I leave a tip?
Karl	I usually leave ten percent. I'm glad you enjoyed the food.
Louise	I had a great evening, thanks.
Karl	No, thank *you* for the meal.
Louise	You're welcome.

Vocabulary

check Rechnung
Don't mention it. Nicht der Rede wert.
I'm full. Ich bin total satt.
Let me get this. Das übernehme ich.
seriously im Ernst

This is on me.
Or: This is my treat.
(not ~~I invite you.~~)

11 Look at the dialogue in exercise 10 again and complete the phrases below.

Phrases

Paying for the meal

Can we get _____¹, please?

Let me _____². / Seriously, this is _____³. / I'll pay for this.

Are you sure? That's _____⁴.

_____⁵ credit cards here?

Do I _____⁶? – I usually leave ten percent.

Thanking your host

I had _____⁷, thanks. / Thank you _____⁸.

Don't _____⁹ it. / You're _____¹⁰.

---

12 Find phrases in the dialogue which mean the following.

1. I enjoyed the meal.
2. I don't want any more to eat.
3. Can we pay, please?
4. I'll pay for this.
5. Really, let me pay for this.
6. That's OK.

Unit 6 . Eating out 39

Key phrases

Here are some key phrases from the unit. Tick the ones that are useful for you.

Talking about what to eat
- [ ] Are you hungry? / How hungry are you?
- [ ] I'm quite hungry / starving.
- [ ] What kind of food do you like?
- [ ] What do you recommend?
- [ ] Do you like Indian/Thai food?
- [ ] I'm vegetarian – will they have a vegetarian option?
- [ ] I don't like spicy food.
- [ ] I can't eat seafood.
- [ ] I don't care much for Indian food.
- [ ] I prefer Italian to Thai food.

Ordering a meal
- [ ] Do you know what you would like for your main course?
- [ ] Are you ready to order?
- [ ] I'll have the soup as an appetizer (AE) / starter (BE).
- [ ] I'd like the venison for my main course – well-done, / medium, / rare, please.

Helping with the menu
- [ ] Can I help you with the menu?
- [ ] Yes, thanks. So what's …?
- [ ] It's a specialty of our region.
- [ ] It's made with cream/meat/fish/vegetables.
- [ ] The meat comes with French fries (AE) / chips (BE).
- [ ] You should try it.

Eating out

Paying for the meal
- [ ] Can we get the check (AE) / bill (BE), please?
- [ ] I'll pay for this. / Let me pay for this.
- [ ] This is on me. / I'll get this.
- [ ] No, it's OK, let me get this.
- [ ] Are you sure? That's very kind of you.
- [ ] Do they take credit cards here?
- [ ] Do I leave a tip? – I usually leave ten percent.

Before and after the meal
- [ ] Enjoy your meal!
- [ ] Cheers!
- [ ] I'm glad you enjoyed the meal.
- [ ] I had a great evening, thanks.
- [ ] That was great, thank you. / Thanks for the meal.
- [ ] You're welcome. / Don't mention it.

You will find an English–German list of these phrases on pages 64–65.

Use this space to write your own useful words and phrases.

....
....
....
....
....

Over to you

13 Think of a situation where you take a visitor for a meal. Is it lunch or dinner, formal or informal? Are you alone or with a group? Write down how you would do the following.

Ask what your visitor likes or doesn't like eating:

....

Offer two or three possible restaurants:

....

Help with the menu in the restaurant:

....

Work with a partner and practice a dialogue in a restaurant. Then change roles and do the activity again. Partner A is the host, Partner B the guest.

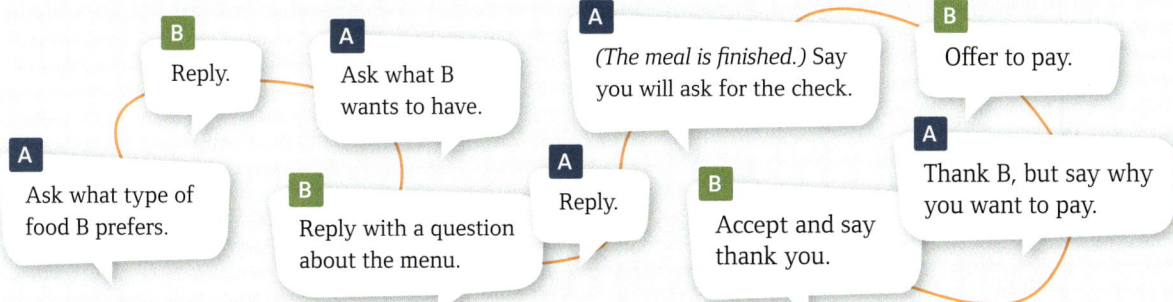

- **A** Ask what type of food B prefers.
- **B** Reply.
- **A** Ask what B wants to have.
- **B** Reply with a question about the menu.
- **A** Reply.
- **A** (The meal is finished.) Say you will ask for the check.
- **B** Accept and say thank you.
- **B** Offer to pay.
- **A** Thank B, but say why you want to pay.

Last but not least

14 Read the article. What are the most important questions for you to think about?

Cultural differences in restaurant etiquette

Understanding restaurant etiquette can help international business people when they eat out. There could be cultural differences: visitors from some cultures don't drink alcohol, for example, or don't eat pork. Don't be afraid to ask if you're not sure.

Think about the following questions:
- Where do you sit – are there rules for who sits where? Is it acceptable for men and women to sit next to one another?
- Body language – how should you sit? Is it bad etiquette to put your elbows on the table?
- Conversation – is this the right place to discuss business?
- The food – who should start eating first? Do you finish everything on the plate? Is it polite to ask for more? Is it rude to leave food on your plate?
- The drink – should you suggest alcohol? If you are the visitor, do you wait for your host to fill your glass?
- Restaurant – who pays for the meal at a restaurant? Could you offend your host by offering to pay?

Vocabulary
acceptable akzeptable, zulässig
elbow Ellenbogen
to offend sb. jdn. beleidigen
polite höflich
rude unhöflich

Talk to your partner about eating out with visitors. Are they usually from different cultures?
Have you ever been to other countries and noticed differences? Is it ever a problem?

Learning objectives
- Talking about the weather
  Über das Wetter sprechen
- Discussing family relationships
  Über Familienverhältnisse sprechen
- Asking about free-time activities
  Sich nach Freizeitaktivitäten erkundigen

7 Making small talk

1 Which of these topics do you talk about informally at work? Which topics are not OK, in your opinion? Do you talk about the same things with male and female colleagues? And with visitors?

work religion health
traffic conditions TV sports
free-time activities money weekends
weather family politics
vacations news

Vocabulary

health   Gesundheit
news   Nachrichten
traffic conditions   Verkehrslage

When did you last talk about one of these topics? Where were you and who were you talking to?

2 Match the words with the pictures.

cloudy · cold · freezing · hot · rainy · stormy · sunny · warm · wet · windy

a 　　b 　　c 　　d 　　e

....　...................　...................　...................　...................

f 　　g 　　h 　　i 　　j

....　...................　...................　...................　...................

Did you know?

The weather is often an easy topic to talk about, especially to start a conversation with people you meet for the first time, or don't know very well.

3 🔊27 Rita is welcoming a visitor from New Zealand. Read and listen to the dialogue. What's the weather like in Munich at the moment?

Rita	Mr. Taylor? I'm Rita Kummer. Pleased to meet you.
Eddie	Good to meet you too. Please call me Eddie.
Rita	Thanks, Eddie. You flew in from New Zealand, right? How was your trip?
Eddie	Fine, thanks. I mean, it's a long flight but it was fine.
Rita	So, have you been to Munich before?
Eddie	No, I haven't. I'm a bit surprised about the weather. Is it normally so wet here?
Rita	Well, actually, the weather is bad this summer. Unusually wet and windy.
Eddie	My bad luck then! I hoped it would be warm and sunny. It's winter in New Zealand.
Rita	Yes, of course. How was the weather back home?
Eddie	It was a beautiful day when I left. But, of course, there was snow.
Rita	Does it snow a lot where you live?
Eddie	In the mountains, yes. Does it get cold here in the winter?
Rita	Oh yes, freezing. Actually, it's really nice if you like skiing and going to the sauna! Luckily, all our meetings are in this building today. We won't have to get our feet wet until we go out to dinner.
Eddie	That's good.
Rita	Oh, perhaps I can get you something now? A coffee or a sandwich?
Eddie	No, I'll be fine, thanks. I ate and slept on the plane.
Rita	OK, if you're sure. This is my office. Would you like to hang your coat up? And then maybe we should begin …
Eddie	Yeah, great, thanks.

Vocabulary
bad luck Pech
to hang up aufhängen
luckily glücklicherweise
unusually ungewöhnlich

4 Look at the dialogue in exercise 3 again and complete the phrases below.

> **Phrases**
>
> **Talking about the weather**
>
> It's very hot/windy/cold here. – You're right. It's lovely/stormy/freezing today.
>
> Is it normally ………………¹ here?
>
> The weather is bad this spring/summer/fall/winter.
>
> What's the weather like where you live?
>
> ……………………………………² back home? – It was ……………………………………³ when I left.
>
> ……………………………………⁴ a lot where you live?
>
> ……………………………………⁵ here in the winter?

In the U.S., people say "fall" or "autumn" for "Herbst"; in Great Britain "autumn".

5 Work with a partner. What can you say about the weather?

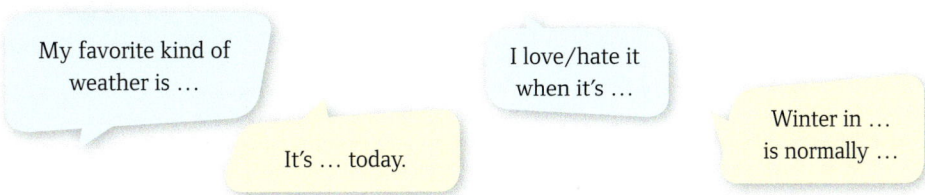

My favorite kind of weather is …

It's … today.

I love/hate it when it's …

Winter in … is normally …

6 🔊 28 Katrina and Judith, two colleagues, are chatting before their meeting. Read and listen to the dialogue. Who is married with no children?

Katrina	Sorry I'm late. I just got a call from one of my kids.
Judith	Is everything all right?
Katrina	Yes, fine thanks.
Judith	How old are your kids now?
Katrina	They're grown up. My son's in college. My daughter is married and has a baby boy.
Judith	A grandson, that's nice.
Katrina	Yes, he's great – nearly six months old.
Judith	And does your son have a partner?
Katrina	He was with a lovely girl, but they separated last year. So, my son's single again now. What about you, Judith? Do you have any children?
Judith	No, I just got married last year. My husband is a chef.
Katrina	Lucky you!
Judith	Yes, he's a great cook. What does your husband do?
Katrina	My ex-husband's a journalist. We're actually divorced now.
Judith	Ah, right.
Katrina	I live with my partner, who's a yoga teacher.
Judith	That's interesting.

Vocabulary

divorced geschieden
to get married heiraten
to separate sich trennen

Did you know?

Some American and British people are more open about their private lives than German people. Don't be surprised if a visitor asks you a question that seems quite personal. When you are chatting to colleagues, it is important to show interest and sometimes to give some extra information to keep the conversation going.

👥 Discuss with a partner if you would have a conversation like this at work.

7 Look at the dialogue in exercise 6 again and complete the phrases below.

Phrases

Discussing family relationships

_____¹ are your kids now?

They're _____² / still in school / in college.

My daughter _____³ and has a baby boy/girl.

They _____⁴ last year.

My son's _____⁵ again now.

My daughter/son has three children.

_____⁶ any children?

I just _____⁷ last year.

What _____⁸ do?

We're actually _____⁹ now.

I live _____¹⁰.

8 Match the questions and answers.

1 Do you have any children?
2 Where does your son live?
3 What does your partner do?
4 What is your daughter studying?
5 How old are your grandchildren?

a They're two and four.
b Economics.
c Yes, two – a girl and a boy.
d He works in IT.
e Not far away.

Work with a partner. Think of ways to keep the conversation going.

> Do you have any children?

> Yes, two – a girl and a boy. They're both teenagers now.

9 🔊 29 Anja and her American visitor are talking about what they do in their free time. Read and listen to the dialogue. What free-time activities do they mention?

Anja   What do you usually do in your free time, Brian? Do you have any hobbies?
Brian I don't have much time during the week. I often work late.
Anja   Same here. So, what do you do on the weekend?
Brian I enjoy being outside, even if the weather's bad.
Anja   Oh, do you like gardening?
Brian No way, I hate gardening! But I love walking and cycling. What about you? Do you do any sports?
Anja   I sometimes go to the gym or do fitness exercises at home. In the summer, I play tennis.
Brian Maybe we can have a game one evening after work.

Vocabulary
even if auch wenn
gym Fitnessstudio

I often work late.
(not I work often ...)
I sometimes go to the gym.
(not I go sometimes ...)

10 Look at the dialogue in exercise 9 again and complete the phrases below.

Phrases

Talking about free-time activities

What do you usually do ....¹?

Do you have ....²? – ....³ during the week.

So, ...⁴ on the weekend?

I like/enjoy/love swimming / going to the theater / watching movies.

I hate / don't like being outside / gardening.

Do you do ....⁵? – ....⁶ to the gym ...

11 Complete the sentences for yourself. Can you find anyone in the class who does the same?

> I sometimes play ...

> On the weekend, I often do ...

> When I have time, I usually go ...

Key phrases

Here are some key phrases from the unit. Tick the ones that are useful for you.

Talking about the weather
- It's very hot/windy/cold here.
- Isn't it freezing/stormy/lovely today?
- Is it normally so wet here?
- The weather's bad this spring / summer / fall (AE) / autumn / winter.
- How was the weather back home?
- What's the weather like where you live?
  – There was snow when I left.
- Does it get cold here in the winter?
  – Oh yes, freezing. / No, not really.

Talking about free-time activities
- What do you usually do in your free time?
- Do you have any hobbies?
- What did you do on the weekend (AE) / at the weekend (BE)?
- Do you do any sports?
- I like/enjoy/love swimming / going to the theater / watching movies.
- I hate / don't like being outside / gardening.
- I go to the gym / play badminton on the weekend.
- I don't have much time during the week.

Activities
play
  badminton, tennis, football, …
  the violin, the piano, the guitar, …
  cards, computer games, …
do
  yoga
  evening classes
  gardening
  homework
go
  jogging
  dancing
  swimming
  sailing
  climbing

Making small talk

Discussing family relationships
- Are you married? – Yes, I got married last year. / No, I live with my partner.
- I'm actually single right now.
- Do you have any brothers/sisters/children?
- How old are your kids?
- My children are grown up / still in school / in college.
- My daughter/son has three children.
- They are separated/divorced now.
- My husband/wife/partner is a banker/cook/…

You will find an English-German list of these phrases on page 66.

Use this space to write your own useful words and phrases.

....

....

....

....

46 English for Socializing and Small Talk

Over to you

12 Think of a situation where you make small talk to someone you don't know, perhaps in a coffee break or before a meeting starts. Write down how you would do the following.

Talk about the weather:

....

Talk about your family:

....

Discuss free-time activities:

....

Work with a partner and practice the dialogue. Then change roles and do the activity again.

A Make a comment about the weather to start the conversation.

B Reply.

B Reply and ask about A's family.

A Ask about B's family.

A Reply.

B Reply.

B Ask if A has any hobbies.

A Reply. Ask what B enjoys doing.

B Reply.

Last but not least

13 Read the question on the problem page. Do you agree with Lydia's advice?

Vocabulary

accidentally aus Versehen
freedom Freiheit
sensitive empfindlich

DEAR LYDIA ... Practical advice for the workplace

Dear Lydia

I work for an international company, and I often travel from Britain to other European countries. I usually find my colleagues are happy to talk about their home life, their families and other personal things. Here in the UK, we often talk about our families, and we even have a "Bring your son or daughter to work" day. But on a visit to Germany, I accidentally offended a young woman by asking her if she was married or had children. Was I just unlucky or are people from northern Europe extra sensitive?

Charlie, Milton Keynes

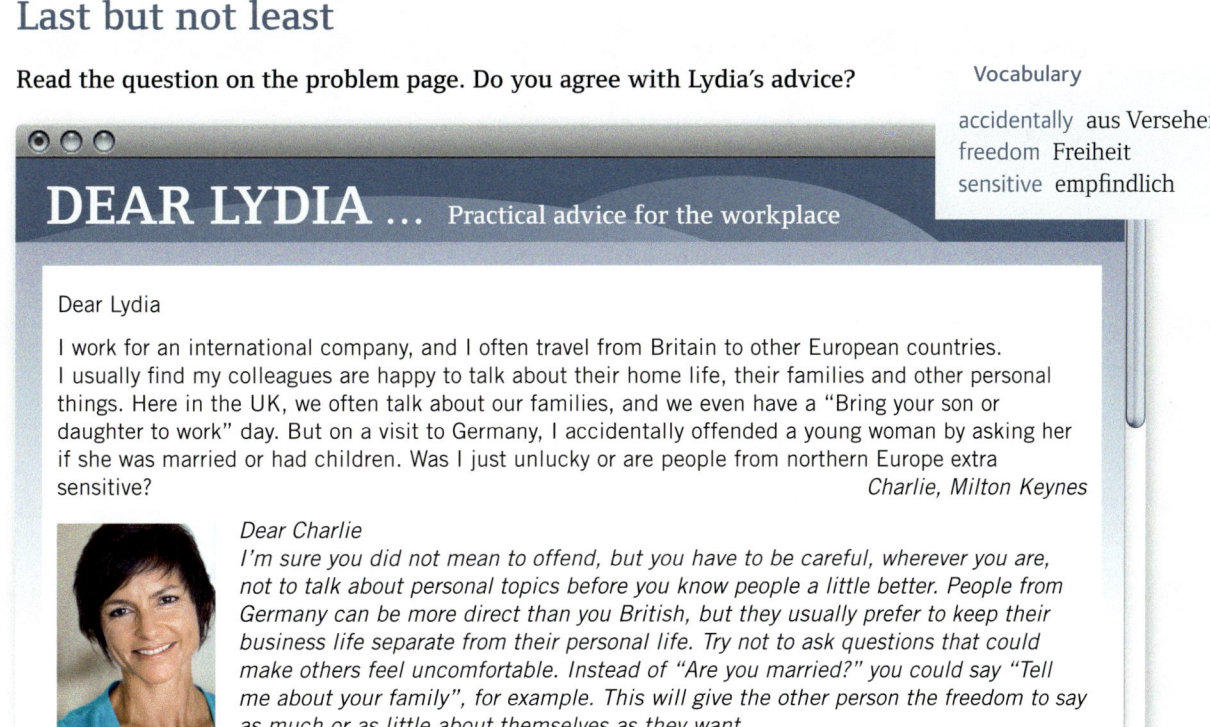

Dear Charlie
I'm sure you did not mean to offend, but you have to be careful, wherever you are, not to talk about personal topics before you know people a little better. People from Germany can be more direct than you British, but they usually prefer to keep their business life separate from their personal life. Try not to ask questions that could make others feel uncomfortable. Instead of "Are you married?" you could say "Tell me about your family", for example. This will give the other person the freedom to say as much or as little about themselves as they want.

Do you ever mix your work life with your personal life? Did your partner in exercise 12 ask you a question you felt was too personal?

Learning objectives
- Beginning/Ending a conversation
  Ein Gespräch beginnen/beenden
- Taking part in discussions
  An Gesprächen teilnehmen
- Talking about what you do
  Über die eigene Arbeit sprechen

8 At a business event

1 Fill out the questionnaire about business events. If you never go to one, find someone in the class who does and ask them the questions.

Which of these business events do you sometimes go to?
trade fair ☐   conference ☐   exhibition ☐   other ☐

What is your role at such events?
an exhibitor ☐   a visitor ☐   an event organizer ☐

Does your company ever have a stand or exhibit at a business event?
Yes ☐   No ☐

Do you ever go to one of the following?
workshop ☐   talk ☐   networking or social event ☐

What language do you normally speak at such events?
German ☐   English ☐   other ☐

Vocabulary

to exhibit ausstellen
exhibition Austellung
exhibitor Aussteller/in
talk Vortrag
trade fair Messe

Compare and discuss your questionnaire with a partner.

2 Starting a conversation with a stranger isn't always easy. Match the parts to make conversation openers.

1 Have you ever been to   a interesting yet?
2 What do you think   b before?
3 Have you seen anything   c if I join you?
4 Haven't we met   d this event before?
5 Do you know many   e of the fair so far?
6 Would it be OK   f people here?

You're at a business event. Practice asking the questions with a partner. How could you answer?

> Have you ever been to this event before?

> Yes, I have actually. I come every year.

> No, this is my first time.

48 English for Socializing and Small Talk

3 ◀30 Bert and Hanna are at a trade fair. Read and listen to the dialogue. Where did they last meet?

Bert   Excuse me, can you help me? I'm looking for *Game-on Publications*.
Hanna I'm not sure, but I think I've seen their stand somewhere here in Hall A. I have some plans of the trade fair – here, take this one.
Bert   Thank you. Haven't we met somewhere before? I'm Bert Yates, from *VideoWorld* magazine.
Hanna Yes, of course! I'm Hanna Schwarz from *Fizz*. But I used to work for *Games-to-Go* in Berlin. Good to see you again. You were at the Games Convention in Leipzig last August, right?
Bert   No, actually I think we met at the E3 Expo in L.A. in June.
Hanna That's right, it was in California. So how are you doing? Do you have a stand here?
Bert   No, I'm just networking. I write reviews for video games so I need to see what's new.
Hanna I see. So, what do you think of the fair?
Bert   Good. Not as big as last year, but personally I think that's an advantage. Smaller fairs aren't as tiring.
Hanna Yeah, I agree. Have you seen anything interesting?
Bert   Not yet, but I just arrived. So, how about coffee or a drink later?
Hanna Excellent idea. My stand's in the center section, you can't miss it. Oh and here's my card.
Bert   Great. And here's mine. Catch you later then.

> **Vocabulary**
> advantage Vorteil
> Catch you later. Bis später.
> review Kritik
> tiring anstrengend

> I used to work for ... = Ich habe früher bei ... gearbeitet.

4 Match the phrases 1–4 with their functions a–d.

1 *Personally, I think* that's an advantage.
2 *So* I need to see what's new.
3 *Here*, take this one.
4 *No actually*, I think we met in L.A.

a offering something to somebody
b politely correcting somebody
c giving an opinion
d giving a reason

5 Look at the dialogue in exercise 3 again and complete the phrases below.

Phrases

Taking part in discussions

Excuse me, can you help me? ....¹ *Game-on Publications*.

– I think ....² somewhere here in Hall A.

........................³ here? – No, I'm just ....⁴.

What ....⁵ the fair?

– Good. Not ....⁶ last year.

Have you seen ....⁷? – Not yet, but I just arrived.

6 🔊 31 **Karen has a stand next to Jan's. Read and listen to the dialogue. How does Karen like her job?**

Jan	Hi there. Can you tell me if Martin Bates is here today?
Karen	Martin has a presentation this morning, but he'll be at the stand again this afternoon. I don't think we've met. My name's Karen Wright.
Jan	Nice to meet you, Karen. I'm Jan Molenaar. I've known Martin for years. Have you worked with him for long?
Karen	No, I just started here. I used to work for *BioWorld* in Bern. I'm head of PR here now, so it's very exciting.
Jan	Congratulations, that's a big job.
Karen	Thank you. What do you do, Jan?
Jan	I work in sales. I've been with *BAM Holding* for two years now.
Karen	Do you travel a lot for your work?
Jan	I'm responsible for the Benelux countries, so yes, there is some travel. I'm from Rotterdam.
Karen	Ah, so that's how you know Martin.
Jan	That's right, we both started at the same company. Our wives became close friends and we went on a lot of vacations together.
Karen	Nice. I'm a long way from home, but I love it here in Europe.
Jan	It's good to hear that …

Vocabulary

close friends enge Freunde/Freundinnen
congratulations Glückwunsch
exciting spannend
head Leiter/in
responsible for zuständig für

> I've known Martin for years.
> (not I know Martin since years.)
> I've been with them since 20.. .
> (not I am with them since 20.. .)

7 Look at the dialogue in exercise 6 again and complete the phrases below.

Phrases

Talking about what you do

I just ....¹. I ....² for *BioWorld* in Bern.

................................³ PR here now.

................................⁴, Jan? – ....⁵ sales.

................................⁶ with *BAM Holding* for two years now / since 20.. .

................................⁷ a lot for your work?

................................⁸ the Benelux countries …

8 👥 Ask your partner some questions about work.

Which company do you work for?

How long have you been there?

I'm with …

I've been there …

English for Socializing and Small Talk

9 Complete the sentences with the correct word from the box.

> for · for · from · in · of · of

1 I'm head .... quality control now.
2 She's never worked .... sales before.
3 They're part .... our R&D team.
4 Who is responsible .... marketing.
5 She came here .... our Spanish branch.
6 He's been in the same job .... ten years.

10 Put the words in the correct order to make questions. Then ask and answer them with a partner.

1 have | lived here | How long | you ....?
2 originally | come from | Where | do | you ....?
3 do | Who | work for | you ....?
4 you | the company | When | join | did ....?
5 do | your job | like | How | you ....?

11 ◁ 32 Listen to Karen talking to three more people at the trade fair. Who does she really *not* want to talk to: Phil, Bella or Ben?

Now answer these questions.
1 Why doesn't Karen go for a coffee with Phil?
2 Why can't she have a drink with Bella?
3 Ben wants to keep Karen talking.
  How does she get away in the end?

12 Listen to the dialogues again. What did you hear?

1
1 a ☐ Sorry, I really have to leave now.
  b ☐ I'm afraid I should really go.
2 a ☐ Let me give you my card.
  b ☐ Can I leave you my card?

2
3 a ☐ Aren't you tired, talking to people all day?
  b ☐ It's tiring, talking to people all day.
4 a ☐ Unfortunately, I have to stay here.
  b ☐ I have to stay here, I'm afraid.

3
5 a ☐ I'm afraid I don't have time right now.
  b ☐ I'm sorry but I'm busy at the moment.
6 a ☐ It was nice meeting you.
  b ☐ It was good to meet you.

> **Vocabulary**
>
> to keep sb. talking das Gespräch am Laufen halten
> unfortunately leider

Do you sometimes find it hard to end a conversation? Tell your partner what you normally say.

13 You're at a business event. Practice ending a conversation with a partner.

> I'm going for a quick coffee. Do you have time to join me?

> I'd love to but …

> Let me tell you more about our products.

> I'm afraid I don't have time right now. I …

Key phrases

Here are some key phrases from the unit. Tick the ones that are useful for you.

Starting a conversation
- ☐ Have you ever been to this event before?
- ☐ What do you think of the fair so far?
- ☐ Have you seen anything interesting yet?
- ☐ Haven't we met before?
- ☐ Do you know many people here?
- ☐ Would it be OK if I join you?

Talking about what you do
- ☐ My name is … and I work for *(company)*.
- ☐ I'm head of PR. / I work in sales.
- ☐ I used to work for *(company)* in *(city)*.
- ☐ I'm part of the marketing team.
- ☐ I just started here.
- ☐ I'm responsible for …
- ☐ I've been in this job for two years / since 20… .

At a business event

Taking part in discussions
- ☐ Do you have a stand here?
  – Yes, we do. / No, I'm just networking.
- ☐ What do you think of the fair?
  – It's very good.
- ☐ Have you seen anything interesting?
  – Yes, it's better than last year. / Not really.
- ☐ Excuse me. Do you know where I can find …? / Can you help me? I'm looking for …
  – Just go to section/hall B.

Ending a conversation
- ☐ Sorry, I really have to leave now.
- ☐ That's very kind of you, but unfortunately I have another appointment.
- ☐ I'm afraid I don't have time right now.
- ☐ Let me give you my card. / Let me take your card and I'll call you.
- ☐ It was good to meet you. / It was nice talking to you.

You will find an English–German list of these phrases on page 67.

Use this space to write your own useful words and phrases.

....
....
....
....
....
....
....

Over to you

14 What phrases could you use at a business event? Write down how you would do the following.

Say something to start a conversation with somebody you don't know:

....

Explain why you don't have time to talk to somebody:

....

Suggest a different time to meet:

....

Tell someone you'll contact them later:

....

Now work with a partner and practice the dialogue. Then change roles and do the activity again. Partner A wants to talk, Partner B is busy and needs to leave politely.

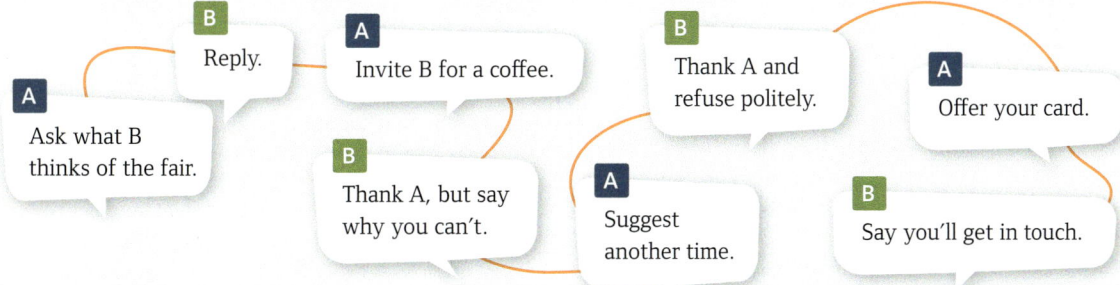

Last but not least

15 Read some advice from a trade magazine.

Networking at a business event

by Sheila Holder

If you are exhibiting at a trade fair, the first impression you make is very important. You want visitors to remember you. Smile and be friendly, and ask open questions to break the ice. Do not start your pitch aggressively. Potential clients can get annoyed, and just walk away. Saying nothing to a visitor is even worse, because you never know – that person could be a big decision-maker. Start with a non-aggressive question like, "What do you hope to get out of the fair?" If the conversation goes well, make a note of anything relevant, exchange business cards and follow up with an email or more information.

Vocabulary

decision-maker
  Entscheidungsträger/in
to follow up anknüpfen
to get annoyed sich ärgern
impression Eindruck
pitch Verkaufsgespräch

Discuss this advice with a partner. Describe a trade fair or business event you have been to. How successful was it for you?

Transcripts

Unit 1 **Exercise 12** ◁07

Greeting a visitor

Erika Mariana Lopez? Welcome to Bonn. I'm Erika Schuster.
Mariana It's very nice to meet you, Ms. Schuster.
Erika Please, just call me Erika. I'm pleased to meet you.

Offering / Asking for help with luggage

Erika You probably had a very early start.
Mariana Oh, not too bad.
Erika You must be a bit tired now. Can I help you with your luggage?
Mariana That's very kind, thank you. Could you take this for me, please?
Erika Sure, no problem. My car's just outside.

Making small talk about the trip

Erika Have you been here before?
Mariana Yes, I have. Several times, in fact.
Erika Really? When were you last here?
Mariana I was here two months ago. I'm looking forward to seeing everyone again.
Erika That's nice. OK this is my car …

Unit 2 **Exercise 11** ◁11

1

Dan Would you like to check into your hotel now, Maria?
Maria Yes I would, thank you. Is it far from here?
Dan No, it's a ten-minute drive.
Maria When's my first appointment?
Dan It's at eleven. It's only 10:30 now, so we could grab a coffee first.

2

Dan I'll pick you up for dinner at six. Is that all right with you?
Maria I need to phone home first, Dan. Can we say half past six?
Dan Sure we can. I'll book a table for seven. Do you like Thai food?
Maria I love it!
Dan Great, me too! So I'll see you at six thirty.

Unit 4 **Exercise 8** ◁18

Linda I hear that Joe's in Basel now, Nick.
Nick Yes, that's right.
Linda Is he still in sales?
Nick Yes, I think so.
Linda Do you know why he left?
Nick Not really. He was a good colleague.
Linda Yes, and he was good at his job too.
Nick I think he works for a phone company now.
Linda Really? Are you still in touch with him?
Nick No, but Mia is. I didn't know him very well, but I liked him.
Linda Me too.
Nick I think he had some problems at home.
Linda Oh, I'm sorry to hear that.

Unit 8 **Exercise 11** ◁32

1

Phil What did you think of that presentation?
Karen It was OK, not great. I thought the speaker was unclear.
Phil Yes, exactly. I'm going for a quick coffee. Do you have time to join me?
Karen I'd love to, Phil but … sorry, I really have to leave now. I'm afraid I have another appointment.
Phil Oh, OK. Well, it was nice talking to you. Let me give you my card.

2

Bella Hi, Karen.
Karen Hi, Bella.
Bella Have you had a lot of visitors at the stand?
Karen Yeah, it's been really busy. I'm getting tired.
Bella I know what you mean. It's tiring, talking to people all day.
Karen Did you make any good contacts yet?
Bella A few. I have a lot of new numbers on my phone. So, how about a drink?
Karen I'd love to, but unfortunately I have to stay here. I'm alone at the stand.

3

Ben Let me tell you more about our products.
Karen I'm afraid I don't have time right now, Ben.
Ben It won't take long.
Karen Sorry, I really must go now. I'm meeting someone in five minutes.
Ben Perhaps you can come back later? I'll be here all afternoon.
Karen Listen, that's very kind of you but I have appointments all day.
Ben How about tomorrow?
Karen Let me take your card and I'll call you when I'm free.
Ben Great. I hope to see you tomorrow, then.
Karen Sure. It was good to meet you.

Answer key

Unit 1

Exercise 1
a 3
b 1, 2, 4

Exercise 2
Helga

Exercise 3
b He is late.

Exercise 4
1 It's good to **see you** again.
2 **I'm fine**, thanks.
3 **Welcome to** Frankfurt.
4 **My name** is Jens Fuchs.
5 It's great to **finally meet** you, Mr. Fuchs.
6 My **pleasure**.
7 I'm **sorry** I'm late.
8 **Don't worry**, it's OK.

Exercise 5
1 c 2 d 3 e 4 a 5 f 6 b

Exercise 6
No, it isn't (her first time in Stuttgart).

Exercise 7
1 a 2 b 3 b 4 a

Exercise 8
1 How **was your trip**?
2 Was the flight **delayed**?
3 No, but I had to get up **very early**.
4 I'm a bit tired, but **I'm OK, thanks**.
5 **Have you ever been here** before?
6 **I was here** three years ago.

Exercise 9
Franz (wants help with his briefcase).

Exercise 10
1 Can I help you with **your bags**?
2 **Let me get** that suitcase for you.
3 **Can I help** you?

Exercise 11
1 Is that your luggage?
2 Can I help you with your bags?
3 Could you take this for me, please? / Could you please take this for me?

a 3 b 1 c 2

Exercise 12
1 b 2 b 3 a 4 b 5 b 6 b

Exercises 13 + 14 (open answers)

Unit 2

Exercise 1 (open answers)

Exercise 2
c Kim needs to freshen up.

Exercise 3
1 Jonas says "great to see you again".
2 The train was cold.
3 He offers her a drink.
4 "Is there a restroom somewhere?"

Exercise 4
1 Do **you need** anything right now?
2 Can **I get you something** to drink?
3 Is there **a restroom** somewhere?
4 Is there somewhere I **can freshen up**?

Exercise 5
1 d 2 a or b 3 a or b 4 c

Exercise 6
b by car.

Exercise 7
1 My car's **in the parking lot** over there.
2 Where **are we going** from here?
3 Is the warehouse **far from here**?
4 We can **get a bus or a taxi** from here.

Exercise 8
1 Where are we going first?
2 Is the office far from here?
3 How do we get there?
4 Is there a train from here?

a 4 b 3 c 2 d 1

Exercise 9
3:00 p.m. Meeting
4:00 p.m. Visit showroom
7:30 p.m. Pick Mrs. Schmidt up.
8:00 p.m. Book table at Italian restaurant

Exercise 10
1 Would you like to **check into** your hotel before your meeting?
2 … we can grab **some lunch** first.
3 You can go **freshen up** in your hotel after that.
4 **Your first meeting** is at 3:00 p.m.
5 We're going to **visit the showroom** at four.
6 And I'll **pick you up** for dinner at around 7:00 p.m.
7 When is my **first appointment**?
8 Could you pick me up **a little later**?

Exercise 11
1 c 2 c

Exercises 12 + 13 (open answers)

Unit 3

Exercise 1 (open answers)

Exercise 2
Theo gives Amanda a visitor badge.

Exercise 3
d A cup of tea with milk.

Exercise 4
1 Lovely **to see you** again.
2 **Welcome to** SynTech.
3 I'll take you **to meet** the team.
4 Can I take **your jacket, Amanda**?
5 **How about** a cup of tea?
6 Here **you are**.
7 Thank you very much. – **Any time**.

Exercise 5
1 Could you wait here please?
2 Can I take you coat?
3 How about a cup of tea?
4 Do you take milk and sugar?

a 1 b 3 c 4 d 2

Exercise 6
Amanda wants to go to the restroom first.

Exercise 7
1 It's **on** the seventh floor.
2 It's **just down the hallway**.
3 Go out of the door and **turn right**.
4 It's the second door **on the left**.
5 It's opposite the photocopier, **next to** the secretaries' office.

Exercise 8
1 next to   2 on   3 at   4 on   5 opposite

Exercise 9 (open answers)

Exercise 10
No, nobody talks about the weather.

Exercise 11
1 Sorry, could you **say that again**?
2 Ah, **you mean** Salim Jaffrey?
3 Sorry, I **don't quite understand**.
4 What **do you mean by** "stuffy" – no fresh air?
5 Could you explain **what you mean**?

Exercise 12
1 c 2 e 3 b 4 a 5 d

Exercises 13 + 14 (open answers)

Unit 4

Exercise 1 (open answers)

Exercise 2
Linda has had contact with Kim and Nick before.

Exercise 3
1 I'd like to introduce **a new colleague**.
2 **This is** Linda.
3 Kim, **have you met Linda** yet?
4 Have you two **met before**?
5 It's good **to see you again**.
6 It's a pleasure **to meet you**.
7 It's nice **to put a face** to the name!
8 I'm **good, thanks**.
9 And **with you**?

Exercise 4
1 d 2 c 3 b 4 e 5 a

Exercise 5
Mia and Linda talk about Tanya and Joe.

Exercise 6
1 How's Tanya **these days**?
2 **Does she still work** at the London office?
3 **How about** Joe?
4 Is he still **with the company**?
5 **What's he doing** now?
6 Are you still **in touch** with him?

Exercise 7
1 on   2 at   3 with   4 in   5 with

Exercise 8
Joe works for a phone company.
1 b 2 a 3 a 4 a

Exercise 9
b Debbie was born in Boston but she lives in Leipzig now.

Exercise 10
1 **Where are you from** originally?
2 **I was born** here in Leipzig, …
3 **I'm from** the States.
4 **Do you miss** America?

Exercise 11
1 e 2 c 3 f 4 a 5 d 6 b

Exercises 12 + 13 (open answers)

Unit 5

Exercise 1 (open answers)

Exercise 2
1 b 2 e 3 f 4 d 5 a 6 c

Exercise 3
Anton suggests going to see a famous church.

Exercise 4
1 Yes, she has.
2 It was too cold.
3 She's interested in historic buildings.

Exercise 5
1 **We could take** a boat trip on the river.
2 That **sounds nice**.
3 Do you have **any more tips** for things to do?
4 There's **a very interesting castle**.

5 **I'd love to** see that, thank you.
6 **I'm interested in** historic buildings.
7 We can go there first **if you like**.
8 That's a **good idea**.
9 **I'd like that** very much.

Exercise 6
1 d 2 e 3 a 4 b 5 c

Exercise 7
Dialogue 1: bistro Dialogue 2: drugstore.

Exercise 8
1 **Can you tell me** where the nearest ATM is?
2 How **do I get there** from here?
3 Excuse me! **I'm lost.**
4 **Is it far?**
5 There's a bar **on the corner of** Königstraße and Pariser Straße.
6 The bank is **on your left** next to the bar.
7 **Go along** Goethestraße …
8 … and **take the first street** on your right.
9 **Turn** right again …
10 … and **you'll see** the hotel on your left.

Exercise 9 (open answers)

Exercise 10
Elisa, Fritz and Brenda are having dinner together.

Exercise 11
1 He doesn't have time. / He's busy.
2 "I'm afraid I don't have time." / "I'm sorry but I'm busy tonight."
3 "That's very kind of you. I'd love to try some traditional German food."

Exercise 12
1 How about **meeting for lunch** today?
2 Would you like **to join us**?
3 We would like **to take you out** for dinner.
4 I'd love to, but I'm afraid **I don't have time**.
5 **I'm sorry but** I'm busy tonight.
6 Perhaps I could **meet you tomorrow**.
7 **That's very kind** of you.
8 **That sounds** very nice.

Exercise 13
1 **How about meeting** for lunch today?
2 **I'm afraid** I don't have time.
3 Would you like to **join us**?
4 **I'm busy** tonight.
5 **Do you have any plans for** this evening?
6 That's **very kind** of you.

Exercises 14 + 15 (open answers)

Unit 6

Exercise 1 (open answers)

Exercise 2
Sally and Karl eat fish.

Exercise 3
1 e 2 d 3 a 4 b 5 c

Exercise 4
1 How hungry **are you**?
2 **What kind of food** do you like?
3 What **do you recommend**?
4 Are you **vegetarian**?
5 **I'm allergic** to it.
6 **Do you like** Indian food?
7 No, I'm afraid **I don't really care for it**.
8 Will they have **a vegetarian option**?
9 **I prefer** Italian to Thai food.

Exercise 5
1 I love seafood but I don't often eat it.
2 I would prefer Italian food because it's not too spicy.
3 I can recommend Marco's because the food is good.
4 I only had a small lunch so I'm starving now.
5 I can't eat nuts because I'm allergic to them.

Exercise 6
Parts of a meal: appetizer, dessert, main course
Types of meat: beef, chicken, lamb, pork
Types of vegetable: cabbage, onion, pepper, potato
Side dishes: French fries, rice, salad
Words for describing food: delicious, savory, spicy, sweet

Exercise 7
Louise chooses *Pfifferlinge in Rahm* and *Hirschbraten mit Spätzle*.

Exercise 8
1 Can I help you **with the menu**?
2 Is that **a type of** meat?
3 It's **a specialty** of our region.
4 It's **made with** cream.
5 You should **try it**.
6 Do you know what you would like **for your main course**?
7 Are you ready **to order**?
8 Yes, **I'll have** the mushrooms …
9 … **as an appetizer**.
10 And **I'd like** the vegetable soup and the pork.

Exercise 9
1 Can I help you with the menu?
2 Yes, please. What's *Kasespätzle*?
3 It's a type of pasta made with cheese.
4 I'll have that as my main course. It sounds good.
5 And do you know what you want as an appetizer?
6 Yes, I'll have the tomato soup.

Exercise 10
Louise pays for the meal because Karl is helping her so much with the new project.

Exercise 11
1 Can we get **the check**, please?
2 Let me **get this**.
3 Seriously, this is **on me**.
4 That's **very kind of you**.
5 **Do they take** credit cards here?
6 Do I **leave a tip**?
7 I had **a great evening**, thanks.

8 Thank you **for the meal**.
9 Don't **mention** it.
10 You're **welcome**.

Exercise 12
1 It was delicious.
2 I'm full. / I've had enough to eat.
3 Can we get the check, please?
4 Let me get this. / This is on me.
5 Seriously, this is on me.
6 Don't mention it. / You're welcome.

Exercises 13 + 14 (open answers)

Unit 7

Exercise 1 (open answers)

Exercise 2
a cloudy b cold c freezing d warm e hot f rainy
g sunny h stormy I wet j windy

Exercise 3
The weather in Munich is wet.

Exercise 4
1 Is it normally **so wet** here?
2 How was the weather back home?
3 It was **a beautiful day** when I left.
4 **Does it snow** a lot where you live?
5 **Does it get cold** here in the winter?

Exercise 5 (open answers)

Exercise 6
Judith is married with no children.

Exercise 7
1 **How old** are your kids now?
2 They're **grown up**.
3 My daughter **is married** and has a baby boy.
4 They **separated** last year.
5 My son's **single** again now.
6 **Do you have** any children?
7 I just **got married** last year.
8 What **does your husband** do?
9 We're actually **divorced** now.
10 I live **with my partner**.

Exercise 8
1 c 2 e 3 d 4 b 5 a

Exercise 9
They mention gardening, walking, cycling, going to the gym, doing fitness exercises and playing tennis.

Exercise 10
1 What do you usually do **in your free time**?
2 Do you have **any hobbies**?
3 **I don't have much time** during the week.
4 So, **what do you do** on the weekend?
5 Do you do **any sports**?
6 **I sometimes go** to the gym …

Exercises 11, 12 + 13 (open answers)

Unit 8

Exercise 1 (open answers)

Exercise 2
1 d 2 e 3 a 4 b 5 f 6 c

Exercise 3
They last met at E3 Expo in L.A., California.

Exercise 4
1 c 2 d 3 a 4 b

Exercise 5
1 I'm looking for *Game-on Publications*.
2 I think **I've seen their stand** somewhere here in Hall A.
3 **Do you have a stand** here?
4 No, I'm just **networking**.
5 What **do you think of** the fair?
6 Good. Not **as big as** last year.
7 Have you seen **anything interesting**?

Exercise 6
Karen finds her job very exciting.

Exercise 7
1 I just **started here**.
2 I **used to work** for *BioWorld* in Bern.
3 **I'm head of** PR here now.
4 **What do you do**, Jan?
5 **I work in** sales.
6 I've **been** with *BAM Holding* for two years now.
7 **Do you travel a** lot for your work?
8 **I'm responsible for** the Benelux countries …

Exercise 8 (open answers)

Exercise 9
1 of 2 in 3 of 4 for 5 from 6 for

Exercise 10
1 How long have you lived here?
2 Where do you come from originally?
3 Who do you work for?
4 When did you join the company?
5 How do you like your job?

Exercise 11
Karen really doesn't want to talk to Ben.

1 She has another appointment.
2 She's alone at the stand.
3 She takes his card and says she'll call him.

Exercise 12
1 a 2 a
3 b 4 a
5 a 6 b

Exercises 13, 14 + 15 (open answers)

Key phrases

Meeting a visitor

Greeting someone you know
Hello, it's good to see you (again).
(It's) Good to see you too.
How are you?
 – I'm fine, thank you. And you?

Jemand Unbekanntes grüßen
Hallo, schön Sie wiederzusehen.
Ich freue mich auch.
Wie geht es Ihnen?
 – Gut, danke. Und Ihnen?

Greeting someone you don't know
James Miller? Welcome to Berlin.
My name is Jan.
It's nice to meet you (, Jan).
 – Pleased to meet you too.
It's great to finally meet you.
 – You too.
It is nice of you to meet me here.
 – My pleasure.

Jemand Unbekanntes grüßen
James Miller? Willkommen in Berlin.
Mein Name ist Jan.
Schön, Sie kennenzulernen (,Jan).
 – Ich freue mich auch.
Endlich lerne ich Sie kennen.
 – Gleichfalls.
Danke, dass Sie mich hier treffen.
 – Keine Ursache.

Saying sorry
I'm sorry I'm late.
 – That's OK.
I am sorry.
 – Don't worry, it's OK.

Sich entschuldigen
Tut mir leid, ich bin zu spät.
 – Kein Problem.
Tut mir leid.
 – Keine Sorge, alles in Ordnung.

Offering help
Are these your bags?
 – Yes, they are.
Can I help you with your suitcase?
 – It's OK, but could you take this briefcase for me, please?
Let me get that for you.
 – No, really, I'm fine, thanks.
 – I can manage, thanks.

Hilfe anbieten
Sind das Ihre Taschen?
 – Ja, sind sie.
Kann ich Ihnen den Koffer abnehmen?
 – Das geht, aber würden Sie die Aktentasche nehmen, bitte?
Ich hole/nehme/mache das.
 – Nein danke, es geht schon.
 – Es geht schon, danke.

Making small talk about the trip

How was your flight/trip?
- Fine, thanks.
- Not so good. The traffic was really bad.

You must be tired now.
- I'm all right, thanks. I slept on the plane.
- I'm a bit tired but I'm OK, thanks.

Have you been here before?
- No, I haven't. I can't wait to look around. / I'm looking forward to seeing the city.
- Yes, I have. I was here three years ago.

Sich über die Reise austauschen

Wie war Ihr/e Flug/Reise?
- Gut, danke.
- Nicht so gut. Der Verkehr war furchtbar.

Sie sind bestimmt müde.
- Ich bin fit, danke. Ich habe im Flugzeug geschlafen.
- Ich bin ein bisschen müde, aber es geht. schon. Danke.

Waren Sie schon mal hier?
- Nein, war ich noch nicht. Ich kann es kaum erwarten, mich etwas umzuschauen. / Ich freue mich schon darauf, die Stadt zu sehen.
- Ja, ich war vor drei Jahren schon mal hier.

Talking about plans

Making visitors feel welcome

Do you need anything right now?
Can I get you something to drink?
Would you like something to drink?

Besuchern das Gefühl geben, willkommen zu sein

Brauchen Sie irgendwas?
Kann ich Ihnen etwas zu trinken holen?
Möchten Sie etwas trinken?

Saying you want to freshen up

Is there a toilet (BE) / a bathroom / ladies' room / men's room / restroom somewhere?
Is there somewhere I can freshen up?

Sagen, dass man sich frisch machen möchte

Gibt es hier irgendwo ein WC / eine Damentoilette / eine Herrentoilette / eine Toilette?
Kann ich mich hier irgendwo frisch machen?

Talking about travel options

My car / The parking lot / The bus stop is over there.
Where are we going from here?
We can get a taxi from here. That's the easiest way to get there.
There's a train/bus in ten minutes.
Is it / the hotel / the office far from here?

Reiseoptionen besprechen

Mein Auto / Der Parkplatz / Die Bushaltestelle ist da drüben.
Wohin gehen wir?
Wir können ein Taxi nehmen. Das ist der einfachste Weg, um da hinzukommen.
In zehn Minuten fährt ein Zug/Bus.
Ist es / das Hotel / das Büro weit von hier?

Explaining the schedule	**Den Ablauf erklären**
Would you like to check into your hotel before the meeting?	Möchten Sie vor dem Meeting im Hotel einchecken?
I'll take you to your hotel.	Ich bringe Sie zu Ihrem Hotel.
We can get/grab some lunch first.	Wir können vorher Mittagessen gehen.
Your first meeting/appointment is at 3:00.	Ihr erstes Meeting / erster Termin ist um 15:00 Uhr.
We're going to visit the warehouse/showroom at 4:00.	Wir besichtigen das Lager / den Ausstellungsraum um 16:00 Uhr.
You can go freshen up in your hotel after that.	Danach können Sie sich im Hotel frisch machen.
I'll pick you up for dinner at around 7:00.	Ich hole Sie gegen 19:00 Uhr zum Abendessen ab.
Is that OK for you?	Ist das für Sie OK?
What time is good for you?	Welche Zeit passt Ihnen?
Asking questions about the schedule	**Fragen über den Ablauf stellen**
When is my first appointment?	Wann ist mein erster Termin?
Could you pick me up a little later?	Könnten Sie mich etwas später abholen?

Welcoming a visitor to the company

Arriving at a company	**Bei einer Firma ankommen**
Lovely to see you again.	Schön, Sie wiederzusehen.
Welcome to …	Willkommen bei …
I'll get you a visitor badge.	Ich besorge Ihnen einen Besucherausweis.
You can leave your things in my office.	Sie können Ihre Sachen in meinem Büro lassen.
Can I take your jacket/coat?	Kann ich Ihnen Ihre Jacke / Ihren Mantel abnehmen?
Would you like a coffee?	Möchten Sie einen Kaffee?
How about a cup of tea?	Wie wäre es mit einer Tasse Tee?
I'll take you to meet the team.	Ich stelle Ihnen das Team vor.
Come this way. / Follow me.	Hier entlang. / Folgen Sie mir.
Thank you very much. – You're welcome. / Not at all. / My pleasure. / Any time.	Vielen Dank. – Gern geschehen. / Kein Problem. / Sehr erfreut. / Jederzeit.
Giving directions around the office	**Wege im Büro beschreiben**
The conference room is on the seventh floor.	Der Sitzungsraum ist in der siebten Etage.
We'll take the elevator (AE) / lift (BE).	Wir nehmen den Aufzug.
It's just down the hallway (AE) / corridor (BE).	Er ist am Ende des Flurs. / den Flur entlang.
It's the first/second door on the left/right.	Es ist die erste/zweite Tür auf der linken/rechten Seite.
It's opposite / next to the mailroom.	Es ist gegenüber vom / neben dem Postraum.
Come with me, I'll show you.	Kommen Sie mit, ich zeige es Ihnen.

Checking understanding	**Verständnisfragen stellen**
Sorry, could you say that again?	Entschuldigung, können Sie das wiederholen?
Do you mean …?	Meinen Sie …?
Sorry, I don't quite understand.	Entschuldigung, ich verstehe nicht ganz.
What do you mean (by …)?	Was meinen Sie (mit …)?
Could you explain what you mean?	Können Sie erklären, was Sie meinen?

Chatting with colleagues

Introducing colleagues	**Kollegen vorstellen**
I'd like to introduce a new colleague.	Ich möchte einen neuen Kollegen / eine neue Kollegin vorstellen.
This is (my colleague) Linda.	Das ist (meine Kollegin) Linda.
She works in R&D.	Sie arbeitet in der Forschung und Entwicklung.
Have you two met before?	Kennt ihr euch schon?
– Yes, we have. It's good to see you again.	– Ja, wir kennen uns. Schön Sie wiederzusehen.
– I think we met in Berlin last year.	– Ich glaube, wir haben uns letztes Jahr in Berlin kennengelernt.
– No, not yet. Pleased to meet you. I'm Paolo.	– Nein, noch nicht. Schön, Sie kennenzulernen. Ich bin Paolo.
– No, but we've had a lot of email contact.	– Nein, aber wir haben schon viele E-Mails miteinander ausgetauscht.
– Good to meet you at last.	– Schön, Sie endlich kennenzulernen.
Welcoming a new colleague	**Einen neuen Kollegen willkommen heißen**
It's nice to meet you. / It's a pleasure to meet you.	Schön, Sie kennenzulernen.
It's nice to put a face to the name!	Schön, Sie endlich mal persönlich zu treffen!
How are you?	Wie geht es Ihnen?
– Very well, / I'm good, thanks.	– Sehr gut, / Gut, danke.
How are things?	Wie läuft es bei Ihnen?
– Good, thanks. And with you?	– Gut, danke. Und bei Ihnen?
Did you find us OK?	Haben Sie gut hergefunden?
– No problem, thanks.	– Ohne Problem, danke.
Talking about people you both know	**Über gemeinsame Kontakte reden**
How's Tanya these days?	Wie geht es Tanya?
Does she still work at the London office?	Arbeitet Sie noch immer bei der Londoner Geschäftsstelle?
How about Joe? Is he still with the company?	Und Joe? Ist er noch bei der Firma?
What's he doing now?	Was macht er jetzt?
Are you still in touch with him?	Haben Sie noch Kontakt?

Talking about where you are from

Where are you from originally?
- I'm from Boston.
- I was born in Leipzig, but I live in Vienna now.

Do you miss America?
- Yes, I do.
- No, I'm very happy here.

Darüber reden, wo man herkommt

Woher kommen Sie ursprünglich?
- Ich komme aus Boston.
- Ich wurde in Leipzig geboren, aber wohne jetzt in Wien.

Vermissen Sie die USA?
- Ja, sehr.
- Nein, ich bin hier sehr glücklich.

Departments

controlling
customer service
HR (human resources)
IT (information technology)
marketing
PR (public relations)
production
purchasing
quality control
R&D (research and development)
sales

Abteilungen

Buchhaltung
Kundenservice
Personalabteilung
IT
Marketing
PR Abteilung
Herstellung
Einkauf
Qualitätsmanagement
F&E (Forschung und Entwicklung)
Vertrieb

Entertaining a visitor

Asking for sightseeing tips

Do you have any tips for things to do?

I'd love to see that, thank you.
That's a good idea. I'd like to do that.

Nach Besichtigungstipps fragen

Haben Sie irgendwelche Tipps, was man machen könnte?
Das würde ich gerne sehen, danke.
Das ist eine gute Idee. Das würde ich gerne machen.

Giving sightseeing tips

There's an interesting museum.
You could take a boat trip on the river.
I can take you there if you like.

Besichtigungstipps geben

Es gibt ein interessantes Museum.
Sie könnten eine Bootsfahrt auf dem Fluss machen.
Ich bringe Sie hin, wenn Sie möchten.

Asking for directions

Where is the nearest ATM?
Excuse me, can you tell me where the bank is?

I'm lost. How do I get to the Imperial Hotel from here?
Is it far?

Nach dem Weg fragen

Wo ist der nächste Bankautomat?
Entschuldigung, können Sie mir sagen, wo die Bank ist?

Ich habe mich verlaufen. Wie komme ich von hier zum Imperial Hotel?
Ist es weit weg?

Giving directions	**Den Weg erklären**
It's opposite the park near the cafe.	Es ist gegenüber vom Park, in der Nähe des Cafés.
It's next to the hotel.	Es ist neben dem Hotel.
Go along this street, then turn left/right.	Gehen Sie die Straße entlang und biegen Sie links/rechts ab.
Take the first/second/third street on your left/right.	Biegen Sie in die erste/zweite/dritte Straße /links/rechts ein.
You can walk from here.	Sie können zu Fuß gehen.

Inviting	**Einladen**
How about meeting for lunch tomorrow?	Sollen wir uns morgen zum Mittag treffen?
Would you like to join us for dinner later?	Möchten Sie nachher mit uns zu Abend essen?
We would like to take you out for dinner.	Wir möchten Sie zum Abendessen einladen.

Accepting or refusing invitations	**Einladungen annehmen oder ablehnen**
That sounds very nice. Thank you.	Das klingt sehr nett, danke.
Thanks, I'd like to do that.	Danke, das würde ich gerne machen.
That's very kind of you. I'd love to.	Das ist sehr nett von Ihnen, ich komme gerne mit.
I'd love to, but I'm afraid I don't have time.	Ich würde gerne mitkommen, aber ich habe leider keine Zeit.
I'm sorry but I'm busy later. How about tomorrow?	Tut mir leid, aber nachher habe ich keine Zeit. Wie wäre es mit morgen?
Maybe we could meet for dinner instead?	Können wir uns stattdessen zum Abendessen treffen?

Eating out

Talking about what to eat	**Sich über das Essen austauschen**
Are you hungry? / How hungry are you?	Haben Sie Hunger? / Wie hungrig sind Sie?
I'm quite hungry / starving.	Ich habe großen Hunger. / Ich bin am Verhungern.
What kind of food do you like?	Was essen Sie gerne?
What do you recommend?	Was empfehlen Sie?
Do you like Indian/Thai food?	Mögen Sie Indisch/Thai?
I'm vegetarian – will they have a vegetarian option?	Ich bin Vegetarier/in – haben sie vegetarisches Essen?
I don't like spicy food.	Ich mag stark gewürztes Essen nicht.
I can't eat seafood.	Ich kann keine Meeresfrüchte essen.
I don't care much for Indian food.	Ich mag indisches Essen nicht sonderlich.
I prefer Italian to Thai food.	Ich mag italienisches Essen lieber als thailändisches.

Helping with the menu	**Die Speisekarte erklären**
Can I help you with the menu?	Kann ich Ihnen mit der Speisekarte helfen?
Yes, thanks. So what's …?	Ja, danke. Was ist …?
It's a specialty of our region.	Das ist eine Spezialität aus unserer Region.
It's made with cream/meat/fish/vegetables.	Es ist mit Sahne/Fleisch/Fisch/Gemüse.
The meat comes with French fries (AE) / chips (BE).	Als Beilage zum Fleisch gibt es Pommes.
You should try it.	Sie sollten es probieren.

Ordering a meal	**Essen bestellen**
Do you know what you would like?	Wissen Sie schon, was Sie möchten?
Are you ready to order?	Sind Sie bereit zu bestellen?
I'll have the soup as an appetizer (AE) / starter (BE).	Ich nehme die Suppe als Vorspeise.
I'd like the venison for my main course – well-done, / medium, / rare, please.	Ich nehme den Hirschbraten als Hauptspeise, durchgegart, durchgebraten/halbgar/blutig.

Paying for the meal	**Das Essen bezahlen**
Can we get the check (AE) / bill (BE), please?	Können wir bitte die Rechnung haben?
I'll pay for this.	Ich bezahle.
Let me pay for this.	Lassen Sie mich zahlen.
This is on me.	Es geht heute auf mich.
I'll get this.	Ich mache das.
No, it's OK, let me get this.	Nein, ist in Ordnung, ich bezahle.
Are you sure? That's very kind of you.	Sind Sie sich sicher? Das ist sehr nett von Ihnen.
Do they take credit cards here?	Akzeptieren sie Kreditkarte?
Do I leave a tip? – I usually leave ten percent.	Gebe ich Trinkgeld? – Ich gebe normalerweise zehn Prozent.

Before and after the meal	**Vor und nach dem Essen**
Enjoy your meal!	Guten Appetit!
Cheers!	Prost!
I'm glad you enjoyed the meal.	Freut mich, dass es Ihnen geschmeckt hat.
I had a great evening, thanks.	Ich hatte einen tollen Abend, danke.
That was great, thank you.	Das war schön, danke.
Thanks for the meal.	Danke für das Essen.
You're welcome. / Don't mention it.	Gern geschehen. / Nicht der Rede wert.

Making small talk

Talking about the weather
It's very hot/windy/cold here.
Isn't it freezing/stormy/lovely today?

Is it normally so wet here?
The weather's bad this spring / summer / fall (AE) / autumn / winter.
How was the weather back home?
What's the weather like where you live?
  – There was snow when I left.
Does it get cold here in the winter?
  – Oh yes, freezing. / No, not really.

Über das Wetter sprechen
Es ist hier sehr heiß/windig/kalt.
Es ist heute richtig kalt / am Stürmen / schön, oder?

Ist es hier immer so nass?
Wir haben diesen Frühling/Sommer/Herbst/ Winter schlechtes Wetter.
Wie war das Wetter zu Hause?
Wie ist das Wetter bei Ihnen?
  – Als ich gefahren bin, lag noch Schnee.
Wird es hier im Winter sehr kalt?
  – Oh ja, eiskalt. / Nein, nicht wirklich.

Discussing family relationships
Are you married?
  – Yes, I got married last year.
  – No, I live with my partner.

I'm actually single right now.
Do you have any brothers/sisters/children?
How old are your kids?
My children are grown up / still in school / in college.
My daughter/son has three children.
They are separated/divorced now.
My husband/wife/partner is a banker/ cook/…

Über Familienbeziehungen sprechen
Sind Sie verheiratet?
  – Ja, ich habe letztes Jahr geheiratet.
  – Nein, ich lebe mit meinem Lebensgefährten / meiner Lebensgefährtin.

Ich bin tatsächlich zurzeit Single.
Haben Sie Geschwister/Kinder?
Wie alt sind Ihre Kinder?
Meine Kinder sind erwachsen / noch in der Schule / an der Uni.
Meine Tochter / Mein Sohn hat drei Kinder.
Sie leben getrennt / sind geschieden.
Mein Mann / Meine Frau / Lebensgefährte ist Banker/Koch/…

Talking about free-time activities
What do you usually do in your free time?
Do you have any hobbies?
What did you do on the weekend (AE) / at the weekend (BE)?
Do you do any sports?
I like/enjoy/love swimming / going to the theater / watching movies.

I hate / don't like gardening / being outside.

I go to the gym / play badminton on the weekend.
I don't have much time during the week.

Über Freizeitaktivitäten sprechen
Was machen Sie in Ihrer Freizeit?
Haben Sie irgendwelche Hobbys?
Was haben Sie am Wochenende gemacht?

Treiben Sie irgendeinen Sport?
Ich mag es / habe Spaß (dar)an / liebe es, zu Schwimmen / ins Theater zu gehen / Filme zu gucken.
Ich hasse / mag keine Gartenarbeit / mag nicht draußen sein.
Ich gehe am Wochenende ins Fitness-Studio / spiele am Wochenende Badminton.
Ich habe unter der Woche nicht viel Zeit.

At a business event

Starting a conversation	**Ein Gespräch beginnen**
Have you ever been to this event before?	Waren Sie schon einmal bei diesem Event?
What do you think of the fair so far?	Was halten Sie bisher von der Messe?
Have you seen anything interesting yet?	Haben Sie schon etwas Interessantes gesehen?
Haven't we met before?	Haben wir uns nicht schon einmal getroffen?
Do you know many people here?	Kennen Sie hier viele Leute?
Would it be OK if I join you?	Ist es in Ordnung, wenn ich mich Ihnen anschließe?
Taking part in discussions	**An Gesprächen teilnehmen**
Do you have a stand here?	Haben Sie hier einen Stand?
– Yes, we do. / No, I'm doing some networking.	– Ja, haben wir. / Nein, ich betreibe Networking.
What do you think of the fair?	Was halten Sie von der Messe?
– It's better than last year's.	– Sie ist besser als letztes Jahr.
Excuse me. Do you know where I can find …? / Can you help me? I'm looking for …	Entschuldigung, wissen Sie, wo ich … finde? / Können Sie mir helfen? Ich suche …
– Just go to section/hall B.	– Gehen Sie in Bereich/Halle B.
Talking about what you do	**Über die eigene Arbeit sprechen**
My name is … and I work for *(company)*.	Mein Name ist … und ich arbeite für *(Firma)*.
I'm head of PR. / I work in sales.	Ich bin der Leiter / die Leiterin der PR-Abteilung. / Ich arbeite im Vertrieb.
I used to work for *(company)* in *(city)*.	Ich habe früher bei *(Firma)* in *(Stadt)* gearbeitet.
I'm part of the marketing team.	Ich bin Teil des Marketing Teams.
I just started here.	Ich habe gerade erst hier angefangen.
I'm responsible for the Benelux countries.	Ich bin für die Beneluxstaaten zuständig.
I've been in this job for two years / since 20… .	Ich arbeite seit zwei Jahren / seit 20.. hier.
Ending a conversation	**Ein Gespräch beenden**
Sorry, I really have to leave now.	Entschuldigung, aber ich muss jetzt wirklich los.
That's very kind of you, but unfortunately I have another appointment.	Das ist sehr nett von Ihnen, aber ich habe leider noch einen anderen Termin.
I'm afraid I don't have time right now.	Ich habe leider im Moment keine Zeit.
Let me give you my card.	Hier ist meine Karte.
Let me take your card and I'll call you.	Geben Sie mir Ihre Karte und ich rufe Sie an.
It was good to meet you.	Es war schön, Sie kennenzulernen.
It was nice talking to you.	Es war schön, mit Ihnen zu sprechen.

A–Z wordlist

A
about (ten minutes)	ungefähr (zehn Minuten)
about, How ~ …?	Wie wäre es mit …?
about, What ~ …?	Was halten Sie von …?
accent	Akzent
to accept	annehmen
acceptable	akzeptabel, zulässig
accidentally	aus Versehen
accommodation	Unterbringung, Unterkunft
activity, free-time activities	Freizeitaktivitäten
actually	tatsächlich, eigentlich
advantage	Vorteil
advice	Ratschlag, Ratschläge
afraid, I'm ~	leider
afternoon, all ~	den ganzen Nachmittag
again	wieder
aggressively	draufgängerisch, offensiv
ago, three years ~	vor drei Jahren
to agree	zustimmen
airport	Flughafen
allergic, to be ~ to sth.	gegen etw. allergisch sein
along, to go ~	entlang gehen
annoyed	verärgert
appetizer	Vorspeise
appointment	Termin, Verabredung
to arrive	ankommen
art exhibition	Kunstausstellung
as if	als ob
to ask about sth.	sich nach etw. erkundigen
at last	endlich, schließlich
ATM (automated teller machine)	Geldautomat
autumn	Herbst
away, to get ~	entkommen, entfliehen

B
bad luck	Pech, Unglück
badge, visitor ~	Besucherausweis
baggage claim	Gepäckausgabe
basic	grundlegend
bill (BE)	Rechnung
bit, a ~	ein bisschen
boat trip	Bootstour
body language	Körpersprache
to book a table	einen Tisch reservieren
born, to be ~	geboren sein
bow	Verbeugung
branch	Zweigstelle, Filiale
break, to take a ~	eine Pause machen
briefcase	Aktentasche, -koffer
building	Gebäude
bus stop	Bushaltestelle
business etiquette	Geschäftsetikette
business partner	Geschäftspartner/in
business trip	Geschäftsreise
business, to discuss ~	Geschäftliches besprechen
business, to do ~	Geschäfte machen
busy	beschäftigt
by (doing sth.)	indem (man etw. tut)

C
cabbage	Kohl
canteen	Kantine
careful	vorsichtig
Catch you later.	Bis später.
cell phone	Handy
center section	Mittelteil
to chat	quatschen, plaudern
check	Rechnung
Cheers!	Zum Wohl!
chef	Koch/Köchin
chilly	frostig, kalt, kühl
chips (BE)	Pommes frites
choice	Wahl
to choose	wählen
climbing, to go ~	Klettern gehen
close friends	enge Freunde/Freundinnen
cloudy	bewölkt
coconut	Kokosnuss
colleague	Kollege/Kollegin
comfortable	bequem, angenehm
comfortable, to be ~	sich wohl fühlen
comment	Kommentar
company	Firma, Betrieb
conference room	Besprechungsraum
Congratulations!	Glückwunsch!
to contact sb.	jdn. kontaktieren
contact, to make contacts	Kontakte knüpfen
to continue	fortsetzen
convention	Tagung
conversation, to keep the ~ going	das Gespräch am Laufen halten
corner	Ecke
corridor (BE)	Flur
cream	Sahne, Rahm
cycling	Radfahren

D
day, all ~	den ganzen Tag
decision-maker	Entscheidungsträger/in
deer	Hirsch
delayed, to be ~	verspätet sein
delicious	lecker, köstlich
department	Abteilung
to depend, It depends.	Es kommt darauf an.
to describe	beschreiben
dessert	Nachtisch
difference	Unterschied
different	unterschiedlich, verschieden
difficult	schwer, schwierig
to direct sb. somewhere	jdn. irgendwohin leiten
directions, to ask for ~	nach dem Weg fragen
directions, to give ~	den Weg beschreiben
dish	Gericht, Speise
divorced, to be ~	geschieden sein
to draw	zeichnen, malen
drive, a ten-minute ~	eine zehnminütige Fahrt
drugstore	Drogerie, Apotheke
during, ~ the week	unter der Woche

E

elbow	Ellenbogen
elevator	Fahrstuhl
embarrassing	peinlich, unangenehm
employee	Arbeitnehmer/in
to end	beenden
end, in the ~	letztendlich
to enjoy sth.	an einer Sache Gefallen finden
enough	genug
especially	insbesondere, besonders
even	sogar
even if	auch wenn
evening classes, to do ~	zur Abendschule gehen
event	Veranstaltung
exchange	Austausch
to exchange	austauschen
exciting	aufregend, spannend
Excuse me!	Entschuldigen Sie bitte!
to exhibit	ausstellen
exhibition	Ausstellung
exhibitor	Aussteller/in
to expand	ausdehnen, wachsen
to experience sth.	etw. erleben
to explain	erklären

F

face, to put a ~ to the name	dem Namen ein Gesicht zuordnen
fall	Herbst
famous	berühmt
far	weit (entfernt)
favorite	Lieblings-
female	weiblich
to fill	füllen
to fill out	ausfüllen
finally	endlich
to finish (a meal)	aufessen
fitness exercise	Fitnessübung
flight	Flug
floor	Etage, Stock
to focus on	sich konzentrieren auf
to follow sb.	jdm. folgen
to follow up	anknüpfen
foreign	fremd, ausländisch
to forget	vergessen
formal	förmlich
free, to be ~ to do sth.	Zeit haben, etw. zu tun
freedom	Freiheit
freezing, absolutely ~	richtig kalt
French fries	Pommes frites
fresh air	frische Luft
to freshen up	sich frisch machen
full, I'm ~.	Ich bin total satt.

G

game, to have a ~	spielen
to get	holen
to get on, How are you getting on?	Wie kommen Sie zurecht?
to get up	aufstehen
glad	froh, erfreut
good, to be ~ at sth.	etw. gut können
government official	Regierungsbeamte/-beamtin
to grab a coffee	sich noch schnell einen Kaffee holen
to grab some lunch	(schnell) Mittagessen gehen
grandchildren	Enkel (pl.)
grandson	Enkel
to greet	begrüßen
greeting	Begrüßung
grown up	erwachsen
gym	Fitnessstudio

H

hallway, down the ~	am Ende des Flurs
hands, to shake ~	Hände schütteln
to hang up (your coat)	(Ihren Mantel) aufhängen
happy, I'll be ~ to …	Ich würde mich freuen, …
hard	schwierig
to hate	hassen, verabscheuen
to have to	müssen
head	Leiter/in
health	Gesundheit
hello, to say ~ from sb.	von jdm. grüßen
here, Same ~.	Das ist bei mir genauso.
historic town center	historische Altstadt
host	Gastgeber/in
HR (human resources)	Personalabteilung

I

I see.	Ich verstehe.
ice, to break the ~	das Eis brechen
immediately	sofort, unmittelbar
important	wichtig
impression	Eindruck
in fact	eigentlich, in der Tat
informal	zwanglos, locker
instead	stattdessen
interest, to show ~	Interesse zeigen
interested, to be ~ in sth.	an etw. interessiert sein
intern	Praktikant/in, Volontär/in
to introduce sb. to sb.	jdn. jdm. vorstellen
invitation	Einladung
to invite	einladen

J K

to join sb.	jdm. Gesellschaft leisten
to keep sb. talking	das Gespräch am Laufen halten
kind	freundlich
to kiss both cheeks	beide Wangen küssen
to know	kennen, wissen

L

language, first ~	Muttersprache
late, to be ~	sich verspäten
leaflet	Merkblatt
to leave	verlassen
to leave sth.	etw. (hinter-)lassen
left, on the ~	links, auf der linken Seite
less	weniger
Let's call it a day.	Lasst uns Schluss machen für heute.
life, home ~	Privatleben
lift (BE)	Fahrstuhl
local specialty	lokale Spezialität
long, It won't take ~.	Es dauert nicht lange.
to look around	sich umsehen

to **look forward to** doing sth.	sich auf etw. freuen	to **order**	bestellen
lost, to be ~	sich verirren/verlaufen	**organizer**	Veranstalter/in
lovely	liebreizend, entzückend	**originally**	ursprünglich
luckily	glücklicherweise	**outside**	draußen
Lucky you!	Sie Glückliche/r!	**over there**	dort drüben
luggage	Gepäck		

M

magazine	Zeitschrift
mailroom	Poststelle
main course	Hauptgericht
male	männlich
to manage	schaffen, bewältigen
map	Karte, Stadtplan
market place	Marktplatz
married, to be married	verheiratet sein
married, to get ~	heiraten
to match	zuordnen, vereinen
may	können, dürfen
maybe	vielleicht
Me too.	Ich auch.
meal	Essen, Mahlzeit
meal, Enjoy your ~.	Lassen Sie es sich schmecken./Guten Appetit.
meat	Fleisch
to meet sb.	jdn. kennenlernen, jdn. abholen, jdn. treffen
to mention	erwähnen, nennen
to mention, Don't ~ it.	Nicht der Rede wert.
menu	Speisekarte
to mind, Do you ~ if I join you?	Darf ich mich zu Ihnen setzen?
to miss	vermissen, verfehlen
mostly	meistens
mountains	Gebirge
to move	umziehen
mushroom	Pilz

N

near	in der Nähe
nearly	fast, beinahe
to need	brauchen, benötigen
to network	netzwerken, sich vernetzen
networking event	Veranstaltung zum Netzwerken
news	Nachrichten
next to	neben
note	Notiz
to notice	bemerken
now, right ~	im Augenblick
now, for ~	im Moment
nuts	Nüsse

O

of course	natürlich
to offend sb.	jdn. beleidigen
to offer	anbieten
office	Büro
on foot	zu Fuß
onion	Zwiebel
opinion	Meinung
opportunity	Gelegenheit, Möglichkeit
opposite sth.	gegenüber von etw.

P

page, problem ~	Kummerkasten
parking lot	Parkplatz
part	Teil
to pay	bezahlen
pepper	Pfeffer
perhaps	vielleicht
personal	persönlich, privat, intim
personally I think …	ich für meinen Teil denke, …
phone call	Telefonanruf
physical contact	Körperkontakt
to pick sb. up	jdn. abholen
pitch	Verkaufsgespräch
plate	Teller
polite	höflich
politics	Politik
popular	beliebt, berühmt
pork	Schweinefleisch
potential	möglich, potenziell
practical	praktisch
to practice	üben
to prefer sth. to sth.	etw. einer Sache vorziehen
probably	wahrscheinlich
problem, to have little ~ doing sth.	keine Schwierigkeiten haben, etw. zu tun
publication	Veröffentlichung

Q R

questionnaire	Fragebogen
quite	ziemlich
R&D (research and development)	Forschung und Entwicklung
to raise	erheben, hochheben
rare	(Fleisch) englisch, leicht angebraten
rather	eher
ready, Are you ~ to …?	Sind Sie bereit um …?
ready, to get ~	bereit sein
receipt	Quittung
receptionist	Mitarbeiter/in am Empfang
to recommend sth.	etw. empfehlen
to refuse	ablehnen
relationship, family relationships	familiäre Verhältnisse
to repeat	wiederholen
to reply	antworten
to respond	antworten
responsible for	zuständig für
restroom	Toiletten
review	Kritik, Rezension
right, on the ~	rechts, auf der rechten Seite
river trip	Bootstour
role	Rolle, Funktion
rude	unhöflich
rule	Regel

S

safe, It's ~ to …	Man kann ohne Weiteres …
sales department	Vertriebsabteilung
same, the ~	der/die/das Gleiche
savory	pikant, appetitlich
scarf	Schal
schedule	Ablauf, Plan
seafood	Meeresfrüchte
to see	ansehen
sensitive	empfindlich, sensibel
to separate	sich trennen
seriously	im Ernst, ernsthaft
server room	Serverraum
set meal	Menü
several times	mehrmals, mehrere Male
shopping, to do some ~	einkaufen gehen
to show	zeigen
to show sb. around	jdn. herumführen
showroom	Ausstellungsraum
shy	schüchtern
side dish	Beilage
sightseeing, to go ~	Sehenswürdigkeiten besichtigen
similar	gleichartig, ähnlich
since	seit
single	alleinstehend
skiing	das Skifahren
small talk, to make ~ about sth.	Small talk machen
social event	gesellschaftliche Veranstaltung
sometimes	manchmal
sorry, I'm ~ / Sorry?	Entschuldigung, das habe ich nicht verstanden, können Sie das wiederholen?
sorry, Oh ~!	Entschuldigung! Das tut mir leid!
sorry, to be ~	bedauern
sorry, to say ~	sich entschuldigen
Sounds good.	Klingt gut.
to speak clearly	deutlich sprechen
speaker, native ~	Muttersprachler/in
to spell	buchstabieren
spicy	würzig, scharf
spring	Frühling
stand	(Messe)Stand
starter (BE)	Vorspeise
to starve, I'm starving!	Ich sterbe vor Hunger.
to stay	bleiben, wohnen
still	noch
stormy	stürmisch
straight	direkt
stuffy	stickig
successful	erfolgreich
to suggest	vorschlagen
suitcase	Koffer
sure	sicher
sure, to make ~	sich versichern
surprised	überrascht
sweet	süß

T

to take part in sth.	an etw. teilnehmen
to take, it ~s 15 minutes	es dauert 15 Minuten
talk	Vortrag
thumb, to have a green ~	einen grünen Daumen haben
time, on ~	pünktlich
to tip	Trinkgeld geben
tip, to leave a ~	Trinkgeld geben
tired	müde
tiring	anstrengend
topic	Thema
touch, to be in ~ with sb.	mit jdm. in Kontakt sein
touch, to keep in ~	in Verbindung bleiben
trade fair	Messe
trade magazine	Fachzeitschrift
traffic	Verkehr
traffic conditions	Verkehrslage
travel	Reise
treat, This is my ~.	Ich lade Sie ein.
tricky	schwierig, heikel
trip	Reise
to try	ausprobieren, kosten
to turn right/left	nach rechts/links gehen
type	Art

U V

uncomfortable	unbequem, unangenehm
understanding, to check ~	Verständnisfragen stellen
unfortunately	leider
unhappy, to make sb. ~	jdn. unglücklich machen
unlucky, to be ~	Pech haben
unusually	ungewöhnlich
upstairs	oben
to use	verwenden, benutzen
used to, I used to …	Früher habe ich …
useful	nützlich
usually	gewöhnlich, normalerweise
vacation	Ferien, Urlaub
valid until	gültig bis
vegetarian	Vegetarier/in
venison	Hirsch, Wildfleisch
visit	Besuch
to visit	besuchen, besichtigen
visitor	Besucher/in

W X Y Z

waiter	Kellner
walking	Spazierengehen, Wandern
warehouse	Lager
way, the easiest ~	die einfachste Möglichkeit
way, this ~	hier entlang
way, to come a long ~	von weit her kommen
weather, to be under the ~	angeschlagen sein
to welcome	begrüßen
well, to look ~	gut aussehen
well-done	(Fleisch) durchgebraten
wet	nass
wherever	wo auch immer
workplace	Arbeitsplatz
to worry	sich Sorgen machen
worse	schlechter, schlimmer
years, for ~	seit Jahren
yet	schon, bereits
yet, not ~	noch nicht

Tracklist

Track	Unit	Exercise	Running time
01	Title/Copyright		0:49
02	Unit 1	Exercise 1	0:53
03	Unit 1	Exercise 2	0:37
04	Unit 1	Exercise 3	0:57
05	Unit 1	Exercise 6	0:57
06	Unit 1	Exercise 9	0:41
07	Unit 1	Exercise 12	1:15
08	Unit 2	Exercise 2	1:01
09	Unit 2	Exercise 6	1:24
10	Unit 2	Exercise 9	1:18
11	Unit 2	Exercise 11	0:51
12	Unit 3	Exercise 2	1:05
13	Unit 3	Exercise 3	0:53
14	Unit 3	Exercise 6	0:41
15	Unit 3	Exercise 10	1:13
16	Unit 4	Exercise 2	1:32
17	Unit 4	Exercise 5	0:45
18	Unit 4	Exercise 8	0:43
19	Unit 4	Exercise 9	1:12
20	Unit 5	Exercise 2	0:29
21	Unit 5	Exercise 3	0:56
22	Unit 5	Exercise 7	1:22
23	Unit 5	Exercise 10	1:08
24	Unit 6	Exercise 2	1:26
25	Unit 6	Exercise 7	1:51
26	Unit 6	Exercise 10	1:15
27	Unit 7	Exercise 3	1:57
28	Unit 7	Exercise 6	1:11
29	Unit 7	Exercise 9	0:49
30	Unit 8	Exercise 3	1:46
31	Unit 8	Exercise 6	1:29
32	Unit 8	Exercise 11	2:09
Total running time			36:25

Studio: Clarity Studio Berlin

Regie und Aufnahmeleitung: Christian Schmitz

Tontechnik: Christian Marx

Sprecher/innen: Tania Carlin, Steve Ellery, Marianne Graffam, Melissa Holroyd, Jeffrey Mittleman, Rikke Mogensen, Lucía Palacios, Helena Prince, Justin Reddig, Dharmander Singh, Ian Smith, Tomas Sinclair Spencer, Simon Srebrny, Clare Wigfall